"*Preparing to Blend* is a kin
are merging two householc
valuable wisdom on this topic ... .g ...-..., ...
in desperate need of. What a gift this book will be to all couples
who want to navigate well and learn to thrive as a stepfamily."

—Lysa TerKeurst, #1 *New York Times* bestselling author;
president, Proverbs 31 Ministries

"As you contemplate creating a blended family, reading and
discussing *Preparing to Blend* is one of the best ways to prepare
for success in creating the blended family that you envision."

—Gary Chapman, PhD, author, *The 5 Love Languages*

"There is absolutely no one better than Ron Deal to help
blended families. No one. This resource is a critical tool in
helping a couple prepare for their future together and the future
of their blended family. Do the critical work now and your kids
will thank you later."

—Dave and Ann Wilson, co-hosts, *FamilyLife Today*

"Ron L. Deal has provided parents and family members with a
hope-filled, practical, timely, and *insightful* resource in *Preparing to Blend*."

—Dr. Tim Clinton, president, American Association of
Christian Counselors; executive director,
James Dobson Family Institute

"This beautifully written book is an extraordinary gift to stepfamilies and to those who want to help them. Ron Deal brings
decades of experience, deep compassion, profound wisdom,
and step-by-step practical guidance to forging a unity of heart
for stepcouples and children journeying through the complexi-
ties of becoming a 'blended family.'"

—Dr. Patricia L. Papernow, author, *Surviving and Thriving
in Stepfamily Relationships* and *The Stepfamily Handbook*

"I view Ron as the leading expert in the world of stepfamily issues. He brings his years of knowledge in the field to this most helpful book. I love it and will recommend it to anyone preparing to blend."

—Jim Burns, PhD, president, HomeWord; author, *Getting Ready for Marriage* and *Doing Life with Your Adult Children*

"Most premarital preparation doesn't foster the needed dialogue to prepare for blending families. But now, *Preparing to Blend* gives couples a roadmap they didn't know they wanted! Ron gifts us with a one-of-a-kind resource from a deep, practical well of decades of focused work counseling blended families and biblical expertise."

—David Robbins, president and CEO, FamilyLife®

"Ron Deal is a recognized expert on blended families; *Preparing to Blend* will equip you to face your future together and blend your family well. It's also a great guide for leaders wanting to offer effective pre-stepfamily counseling. I highly recommend it."

—Shaunti Feldhahn, social researcher; bestselling author, *For Women Only*, *For Parents Only*, and *Thriving in Love & Money*

"What are the practices and considerations couples should prioritize as they prepare for remarriage? Ron Deal is a foremost authority on blended families, and he has written an indispensable manual for engaged couples who want to successfully blend their two families."

—Jim Daly, president, Focus on the Family

"I thank God for Ron Deal! His advice is so practical, real to life, wise, and helpful. This will be my go-to book to give to couples who are about to blend their families."

— Gary Thomas, author, *Sacred Marriage* and *Sacred Parenting*

"Many books on blended families focus more on helping parents and minimize children's needs. *Preparing to Blend* boldly dives deeper into the struggles of family members. This is a powerful, effective, and easy-to-follow roadmap for every blended family. If you want a healthy and strong blended family, *Preparing to Blend* is a must-read."

—Meg Meeker, MD, bestselling author,
Strong Fathers, Strong Daughters

"Ron Deal's expert voice and years of experience provide a travel guide of wisdom through the issues of blending a family, such as what to expect, why it's different, how to handle unhappy kids, setting boundaries, the former spouse, jealousy, discipline, bonding, loyalty, and other issues that can cause conflict. *Preparing to Blend* is a must-read for blending couples, extended family, pastors, and therapists. I highly recommend this resource."

—Laura Petherbridge, speaker, author

"Ron Deal has studied and assisted stepfamilies for decades and knows more about them than anyone ministering to them today. *Preparing to Blend* needs to be required reading for any two people wanting to marry and blend their families."

—Steve Arterburn, bestselling author
and founder of New Life Live

"If you want to prepare yourself adequately to blend a family, read this book. Ron Deal has identified relational dynamics and everyday scenarios of stepcouples that prepare you for the road ahead and how to navigate it. Whether your kids are young, teenagers, or adults, this book is for you."

—Gayla Grace, staff writer for FamilyLife®; author,
Stepparenting with Grace

"*Preparing to Blend* is Ron Deal's crowning jewel! Packed with practical application for couples entering the stepfamily journey! You'll be delighted as a pastor, counselor, or one who is remarrying to heed the guidance in these pages. Knowing how to navigate the pain one has come from increases the success of remarriage legacy."

—Gil Stuart, MA, LCHMC, and Brenda Stuart, CTC, coauthors, *Restored and Remarried*

"Every couple who is preparing for married life in the proverbial blender needs all the help they can get. And Ron Deal is *the* expert on the topic. He writes with knowledge, compassion, and a wealth of practical insight. We'll be recommending this book for many years."

—Drs. Les & Leslie Parrott, #1 *New York Times* bestselling authors, *Saving Your Marriage Before It Starts*

PREPARING TO
BLEND

SMART
STEPFAMILY
SERIES

Books in the SMART STEPFAMILY SERIES

PREPARING
TO
BLEND

The Couple's Guide to
Becoming a **Smart** Stepfamily

RON L. DEAL

BETHANYHOUSE
a division of Baker Publishing Group
Minneapolis, Minnesota

© 2021 by Ron L. Deal

Published by Bethany House Publishers
11400 Hampshire Avenue South
Bloomington, Minnesota 55438
www.bethanyhouse.com

Bethany House Publishers is a division of
Baker Publishing Group, Grand Rapids, Michigan

Printed in the United States of America

Library of Congress Cataloging-in-Publication Data
Names: Deal, Ron L., author.
Title: Preparing to blend : the couple's guide to becoming a smart stepfamily /
    Ron L. Deal.
Description: Minneapolis, Minnesota : Bethany House, a division of Baker
    Publishing Group, [2021] | Includes bibliographical references.
Identifiers: LCCN 2021025321 | ISBN 9780764237935 (paper) | ISBN 9780764239694
    (casebound) | ISBN 9781493433551 (ebook)
Subjects: LCSH: Stepfamilies. | Marriage counseling. | Families.
Classification: LCC HQ759.92 .D38 2021 | DDC 306.874/7—dc23
LC record available at https://lccn.loc.gov/2021025321

Cover design by Eric Walljasper

Author represented by MacGregor Literary

Baker Publishing Group publications use paper produced from sustainable forestry practices and post-consumer waste whenever possible.

21 22 23 24 25 26 27   7 6 5 4 3 2 1

*To those who have loved and lost
and are willing to try again.
May coupleness be your haven
and familyness be your crowning joy.*

Contents

11

Acknowledgments

This book is the culmination of a multi-book partnership with Bethany House Publishers (special thanks to Andy, Ellen, David, Steve, Holly, Deirdre, Eric, Julie, and Jim) and the guidance of my agent, Chip MacGregor. What fun it has been working with all of you to bring peace to couples and families.

Special thanks are also due to the leadership of FamilyLife®, our key donors for seeing the need for stepfamily education and support, and to my current FamilyLife Blended® team and bonus "adjuncts": Lynn and Larry, Gayla, Nicole, Kevin, Ann, Julie, Debbie, Sabrina, Tim, Kim, and Shannon.

And to my bride, Nan. Since 1986, the roller coaster we've ridden together has been full of ups and downs, sweet intimate vistas, and bitter sorrowful valleys. And through all of it, your love and partnership has given me a safe place to grow, mature, research, and share with others. I cannot thank you enough or thank God enough for you.

Introduction

This email is typical of the ones I frequently get through my website SmartStepfamilies.com.

> Hi Ron. A few years ago, I lost my wife of 34 years. We had two sons together and a wonderful family. Now there is a new love in my life. She lost her husband four years ago, has two children in their mid-twenties, and one grandchild. We're planning to get married but want to start this family off right. We're reading your books and listening to your podcast but think premarital counseling with someone who understands blended families well would be wise. Can you help us?

Yes, I can help them. And I can help *you.*

Many couples reading this are engaged and making wedding plans. (For the most part, I'm going to assume you're either engaged or are considering it. If you're not serious about engagement yet, you might read my book *Dating and the Single Parent*, then come back to this one.) This is an exciting time for you. But engagement is not just about planning a wedding; it's about planning for your marriage and blended family after the wedding. That's the focus of this book—to help you

Even though research confirms that premarital preparation strengthens relationships, most couples forming blended families don't seek it out.[1] Obviously, that's not you. *Good for you.*

continue the "family merger" you've already started and gain relational strength as you move toward the wedding. I've spent three decades working with families and developing resources specifically for blended families; it will be an honor to come alongside you as you prepare for the big day and what follows.

In case you're wondering, this book is appropriate for couples with young children and those with adult children, for those with a full nest and those with an empty nest. It's applicable if one or both of you are bringing biological children to the picture (and if you have a child together), and if death, divorce, or a dissolved relationship preceded your falling in love. Yes, stepfamilies come in many shapes and sizes—and I've tried to consider all while writing this book. Not every section will apply specifically to you, but most will.

In some ways this book is a continuation of the book I just mentioned, *Dating and the Single Parent*. If you read that book while dating, I'll pick up where it left off. If you're already engaged and didn't read it, that's okay. I'll integrate a few of the relevant points in this book. Now, having said that, if you are interested in learning more about any of the following topics, you may want to pick up a copy of that book since these are not covered in this one:

- Wise dating practices that consider children's emotional needs;
- Relational dynamics surrounding cohabitation before marriage;

- Questions about divorce and remarriage from a Christian perspective;
- How to know with confidence if forming a blended family is a good decision for you and the kids at this point in time.

This book assumes you are already headed toward the altar, but even then, preparing to form a blended family sometimes causes people to want to take a step back and explore the above topics. *Dating and the Single Parent* will help you do that.

Surround Yourself

In the early 1990s, when I first started working with stepfamilies, people would complain to me, "Ron, where are all the resources for blended families?" and they were right to do so. Practical resources for the general public were few and far between. But that's not true anymore. To date I have published more than a dozen resources and served as author and consulting editor of a series of books (SMART STEPFAMILY SERIES) for stepmoms, stepdads, and dating and married couples on a variety of subjects (e.g., money management and stepparenting), as well as multiple video curriculum and hundreds of online articles and videos. In addition, I'm teaching virtual classes, working with organizations and experts that cumulatively have produced many additional resources, dozens of national radio broadcasts, my popular podcast *FamilyLife Blended*, and worldwide on-demand livestream training. You can and should surround yourself with this trusted, research-informed, on-demand content, all accessible at SmartStepfamilies.com. Absorb as much of it as you can and decide now to be a student of stepfamily living. The more you know, the smarter you are, and the healthier your family gets.

General books on marriage can be helpful to you as well. For example, this book is a sister book to *Preparing for Marriage*, which is primarily for couples without children, getting married for the first time. That book lays an important Christian foundation for the purpose of marriage, describes various roles we play within marriage, and discusses healthy and unhealthy expectations for marriage. (I will not take the time to address those subjects here since that book does.) Another complementary resource is my book *The Smart Stepfamily Marriage*, coauthored with Dr. David Olson. Based on the largest survey of couples creating stepfamilies ever conducted, it includes an online relationship profile that provides personalized feedback about your relationship as you learn communication and conflict resolution skills, and gain insights about your relational styles, expectations, personalities, leisure preferences, sexual expectations, desired spiritual connection, and parenting strategies. It is a comprehensive examination of marriage in a blended family that can be read before or after the wedding and will complement what you find here.

Practical and Proven

In addition to emails like the one beginning this introduction asking if I can help prepare a couple for marriage in a blended family, I have also received thousands of emails, podcast reviews, and social media messages from couples who have been married for twenty years or more, thanking me for helping them navigate their family journey. The principles discussed in this book are practical and proven. However, if there's one truth about life, it's that none of us get to control it; no one can give you a recipe that will allow you to make every relationship just the way you want it. But having said that, I do know a few things that will help. I invite you to read this book with an open heart and mind. But don't just read it. *Do it.* That brings me to the central engine of this book, Growing Activities. Do them and you will be forever changed.

NOT JUST A COUPLE

Growing Activities, Bonding, and Becoming a Family

When it comes to blended families, *coupleness* does not necessarily equal *familyness*.

Right now you're a couple. The focus of your romantic love, and likely most of your dating, has been on falling in love and building a vision for your life together. But becoming a blended family involves so much more than just the two of you.

This book centers around several key Growing Activities that are designed to help you take steps toward family bonding—not just talk about familyness, but actually move toward it. So no, you can't read the chapter discussion and skip the activity. If you want to get the most from this book, you need to do the Growing Activities and include the children when indicated. I'll say more about the design of the Activities in a moment, but first I want you to consider something.

Join one of my virtual pre-blended family education groups for engaged couples at SmartStepfamilies.com.

Even though this book is DIY (do-it-yourself) pre-stepfamily training, I recommend you include one other person. As someone who has spent thousands of hours counseling and coaching couples, my advice is that you walk through the pages of this book with a relationship mentor, coach, or pastor. The best athletes, managers, salespersons, and even therapists have someone watch and coach them as they learn their craft. Sitting with someone who can ask probing questions and comment on your couple and family relationship dynamics will multiply the insights you gain and the ways you apply the wisdom of this book. I highly recommend that you take the time to find someone to walk with you. At SmartStepfamilies.com you can join my virtual groups for engaged couples and find a list of recognized Smart Stepfamily Therapy Providers™ (professionals who have been through my therapy training) who offer coaching and therapy to couples. In addition, many local places of worship offer premarital counseling. And organizations like Prepare-Enrich.com and SYMBIS.com can point you to certified coaches who make use of their online relationship assessments (which I highly recommend; you'll even find some of my Smart Stepfamilies material integrated into their resources).* Organizations like FamilyLife.com (I started the division called FamilyLife Blended®) and ForYourMarriage.org (Catholic Family Ministries) offer general marriage training, events, and small groups for couples, and FamilyLife.com/blended has a searchable map to help you find blended family ministries and

*Prepare-Enrich has a parenting assessment that I find especially helpful to blended family couples.

events around the country. You can walk through this book on your own, but I recommend you don't. Find a trusted guide who can walk beside you.

And in case you're wondering, making time for premarital preparation with a trusted guide is extremely valuable for couples in general. Numerous studies show that it really works. One study found that premarital preparation can reduce the risk of divorce by 30 percent.[1] Another meta-analysis of multiple studies found that overall, couples showed 79 percent improvement in all marital outcomes compared to couples who did not receive premarital education.[2] Taking the time to invest in your coupleness clearly matters.

Now, here's the catch: There are tons of pastors and marriage mentors or coaches, but not many have taken the time to become familiar with the unique dynamics of stepfamilies. Since you need to learn how to be a strong couple and a strong family, you need premarital preparation designed specifically for blended families. Go to the wrong coach, and you could end up getting misguided advice. My work trains and equips them for working with blended families, but many are still unfamiliar with it. So I've written this guide as a tool that can inform both you and them. Walking with them through each chapter, doing the Activities, and having the discussion will educate both of you and enhance your application of the material.

To the Pastor, Coach, or Mentor:

Use this book as your premarital counseling program and help close the gap in premarital education for blended family couples. A free downloadable guide is available along with suggestions for conducting blended family weddings. Go to FamilyLife.com /preparingtoblend.

Why Growing Activities?

If you want to make a new friend or deepen a romantic relationship, you must engage one another in a way that transforms the relationship. You can't just talk about having a better relationship; you have to do things *together* that make the relationship better and raise your emotional quotient.

The Growing Activities in this book are designed to move your step-relationships forward. Each chapter explains what the corresponding Growing Activity is meant to accomplish and why it is important to your family. Instructions for doing the activity are then outlined, and follow-up questions will help you process what you learned, identify insights gained from the Activity, and determine what steps your family might take next. Processing these questions with your mentor or pastor is wise as well.

Becoming family to one another—which is fundamentally what every blended family is hoping to accomplish—is an emotional process that requires active engagement by all parties. You can't just wish stepchildren, for example, into accepting, respecting, or loving a stepparent. They must develop mutual trust and affection through actual interaction. Growing Activities are intended to either move you in that direction or reveal what is standing in the way.

If you read *Dating and the Single Parent*, you may recognize a couple of the Activities. Even if you have done the Activities before, go through them again. Life and relationships are like a flowing river. You are further downstream than you were the first time you had the conversation, so go ahead and enter the stream again. You may find the outcome is different for a variety of reasons. Trust the process and jump in.

Include the children. It is critical that you include the children in Growing Activities when indicated. For years I've believed that children who feel included in decisions related to forming a blended family and can speak into the process find embracing the new family easier than children who aren't, and there's evidence of that. Researchers examining the importance of involving children in blended family educational courses concluded, "When it comes to strengthening couples in stepfamilies, the involvement of children is clearly implicated and should not be underestimated."[3] Here's why. The loss (actually, the *series* of losses) that children of every age experience leading up to a parent's marriage steals a sense of control and influence over their own lives. Anything you do to give them some voice in what's about to happen—and how it happens—restores some of that and may shift them from being a victim of their circumstances to a contributor to what is being built. And being a contributor makes it more likely they'll follow through with their part of the plan, because the message they receive from being included is that they are valued and important. Therefore, kids of all ages need some input into their future family; the Growing Activities help them do that in a tangible way.

By contrast, when children aren't involved in the planning, can't relate to the style of your wedding ceremony, or feel the ceremony dishonors their original family, they may experience your wedding as empty and meaningless.[4] To help you design a pre-wedding journey and family-based ceremony that is full of meaning and fosters family identity, chapter 4 goes into great detail about what is helpful to children of every age. By the way, if you are currently planning your wedding (e.g., the date and the details of the ceremony itself), you may want to skip to that chapter sooner rather than later so you can plan with wisdom. And share that chapter with your pastor, who likely also needs a little education about designing a blended family ceremony.

Giving children a voice in decisions that are affecting their lives and the family is important, but the most important reason you must include the children in Activities is that they need relational reassurance from their biological parent that they haven't been forgotten. Children are highly invested in maintaining relationship with their biological parent(s). When their mom or dad falls in love and gives their time and energy to another adult, it is natural for them to feel pushed aside, insignificant, and vulnerable. You need to move toward your children so you can move toward your new spouse. Therefore, it's wise from time to time when engaged in the family-centered Growing Activities for the future stepparent to step back and, for example, let the biological parent take the lead on the Activity or even have exclusive time with their kids to complete the Activity. You'll have to decide when to include the future stepparent and when not to, but occasionally compartmentalizing relationships in this way paradoxically helps children include the stepparent; when they are reassured of their parent's continued love and presence, children feel less relationally threatened by the stepparent (and perhaps new stepsiblings) and are more likely to open their hearts to them.

Some Growing Activities are couple-centered, others family-centered. In the end, the Activities aim to create for you three combinations of time together: biological parent-child time, couple time, and "family time" when the stepparent (and their children) are included. Even after the wedding, strive to keep this balance of time throughout your first few years. It feeds each person and helps prevent relationships from competing.

One more thought: In times of stress (whether caused by life events or the transition to a blended family), it is helpful for biological parents to increase parent-child alone time and decrease family time (while still maintaining couple time to continue nurturing the marriage in the midst of family stress).[5] This can feel to stepparents like they are being excluded, but long-term it has the opposite effect. When children feel safe with their biological parent, they are more open to the stepparent, not less.

Building memories and a common language. Another advantage of the Growing Activities is that they build memories that the family can refer to after the wedding. For example, drawing your digital Blended Family Map (chapter 2) and helping to plan the wedding (chapter 4) create fun memories that stand on their own and represent the process of becoming a family. Positive memories serve a bonding function, and they give everyone a common language that they can utilize as they move through time. "Do you remember when we made that family map? I'll never forget realizing how hard it must be for Ashleigh to spend time with me when she can't be with her biological parent." Observations like this become points of mutual understanding that move individuals along the path of becoming family to one another.

Full steam ahead? By the way, if you experience significant resistance from children during the Growing Activities, you need to, at a minimum, spend more time and energy working through the barriers, and at a maximum, consider slowing your roll toward marriage. Children shouldn't get to dictate if and when you marry, but unwise is the couple who ignores the pushback or distress evident in a child(ren). Moving forward despite that is equivalent to shooting yourself in the foot. Instead, slow down. Talk through what you're seeing and what it tells you about the child. Consult with your mentor or coach (or small group), and together decide how you will move forward.

If, on the other hand, your Growing Activities experience affirms your wedding plans, full steam ahead.

Getting Started

I suggest that each of you read a chapter and discuss the concepts and the Growing Activity as outlined. Some couples will want two copies of this book in order to highlight what speaks to them most; others will share a copy. If you have a mentor or coach, you can discuss the chapter with them before and after doing the Activity (this makes a good structure for pre-stepfamily counseling). Feel free to modify the Activity for your family based on the ages of your kids, how well people are getting along, visitation schedules, and how much time you have. Make it your own. And if any Activity feels too risky, for whatever reason, feel free to skip it, but be sure to talk with each other and your coach about your concerns. What feels risky about it? What are you afraid will happen? These questions can be quite revealing.

After each Activity, share what you observed, what you think it means, and the implications for your journey forward. Each Activity is both an intervention—meaning it is designed to advance your family bonding process—and an assessment device—meaning it provides a feedback loop of information you didn't have before the Activity. Be sure to incorporate that information into how you move forward. For example, celebrate when you feel confirmation about the attitude of children or the family journey in general, and slow down to process information that suggests someone is struggling more than you realized.

Finally, let me make a comment about the order of the Growing Activities. There is a method to my madness. Activities—and the insights they bring—build on one another, so it's best if you go in order. The exceptions to that are "Planning Your Wedding" (chapter 4) and "Merging Money and Your Family" (chapter 9), which can be done at any point.

Co-Creating Your New Family

Unless you met as strangers on the TV program *Married at First Sight*, you have probably spent hundreds if not thousands of hours investing in your coupleness. And if you had a few dating growing pains, keep in mind there were only two of you. You now endeavor to merge the lives of multiple children, sometimes from multiple homes, with perhaps a couple dozen extended family members for the rest of your lives. Let's just do the math, shall we? Biological families are often comprised of two parents and four grandparents. That means there are six primary parent figures directly responsible for childrearing and nurturing children through their lives—all of whom have a direct biological tie to a child who very much wants them in their world. Blended families often have between three and seven parents and stepparents, across three or more households, plus eight or more sets of grandparents, totaling nine to twenty-one parent figures. Now, keep in mind that many of these people don't like each other—which, of course, makes parenting far more complicated and difficult—and that on day one, children have strong preferences that some parent figures remain in their world while they would be fine with or without others. If you have invested hundreds or thousands of hours in building your coupleness, don't you think you need to be just as intentional *with children* to co-create your familyness? Let's get started.

TRY THIS

As you launch into this book, I encourage you to start a one-minute daily habit that will connect you and your spouse.

My one-year devotional *Daily Encouragement for the Smart Stepfamily* (with Dianne Neal Matthews) offers simple, practical thoughts to guide your journey to becoming family. Reading each day's thought literally takes less than a minute but can ignite important discussions as you strengthen your marriage and co-create your relationships and vision for parenting. And here's the bonus benefit: Reading that book on a regular basis, even as you work through *Preparing to Blend*, will establish a value-centered relationship habit that will stay with your relationship throughout the years. Now, *that's* a habit worth beginning.

2

SEEING IS EYE-OPENING

Drawing Your Blended Family Map

For close to thirty years in both individual therapy and large conferences, I've been using a tool familiar to family therapists called a genogram to help couples see the complexity of their blended family. Seeing is eye-opening. And when you do your family map, it is revealing, insightful, and hope-giving. Revealing because it removes the blinders romantic love has placed on your eyes so you can see the vast number of connections, dynamics, and factors affecting your family. Insightful because it helps you visualize the underlying relational dynamics that move your family through time and space. And hope-giving because the insights you gain empower your journey together as a family.

After completing their genogram and seeing how complex their multi-generational, multi-household family really is, I've had a few couples lose some optimism; instead of giving them hope for their future, they tell me I'm trying to crush their dreams.

But it's just the opposite! I'm trying to help you climb a mountain, together, with your eyes open. Romantic love, whether it's your first love or fifth, literally puts your brain in a kind of chemical daze. It reduces the activity of the frontal lobe (the part of your brain that actually thinks) and activates the parts of your brain that light up when someone is on cocaine. No, I'm not kidding. Let me put it this way. The Rocky Mountains look pretty small from a hundred miles away. It's easy to say, "Oh, that's nothing. We can climb that in no time." Romantic love makes you view building a new family that way. But move to the base of the Rockies and your eyes are opened. Climbing to the top might take a little more time—and the path may be steeper—than you thought. That's my job; to move you to the base of the mountain. For three decades, blended family couples have complained to me, "Why didn't anyone tell me this before we married?" Well, I'm telling you before you marry.

At this point, your heart may be racing a bit and you may feel like you're about to hear bad news. That's not the case. You're just going to hear truthful news—some of which will be encouraging, while some may challenge your assumptions about the climb. Either way, if I may borrow a phrase: The truth will set you free. Hope is found in an honest appraisal of your circumstances. Blind hope is no hope at all.

Your Digital Blended Family Map

My friends at Blending.Love have created a digital genogram that you can do online; they call it a Blended Family Map. Like a genogram commonly used by family therapists, a Blended Family Map can help you examine your family history, relationship patterns and roles, ethnic influences, and the unspoken rules for family behavior. In addition, you can use your digital map to anticipate how your family will look and interact after the wedding. Questions provided in this chapter (and throughout the book) will help reveal some of this, but much of this exploration you can do on your own just by being curious and asking each other questions. Plus, working with a pastor or counselor who is familiar with genograms can open your eyes even more as they ask probing questions.

Before they met, Juan and Hailey had each been married and divorced. Juan grew up in a first-generation immigrant Mexican family that very much valued traditional Hispanic family culture. His first marriage was to Maria, a woman with similar family values. They had three children together: Mia, Aria, and José. Juan and Maria would each tell you that they divorced simply because they grew apart, though Maria would add that she tried to save the marriage more than Juan did. Today, Maria, who is still single, lives just a few miles from Juan, and both sides of their extended family live nearby as well. Their children visit grandparents often and move regularly between their two homes; as former spouses who highly value a close extended family (a Hispanic cultural value known as familism), Juan and Maria have a fairly cooperative co-parenting relationship.

Hailey, a Caucasian woman from the Midwest, grew up in a single-parent home. Her father left her and her two brothers when she was young and continues to be an unpredictable presence in her life. Just before graduating from college, Hailey got pregnant with her daughter, Emma (now age fourteen). She married the father (Cameron) and had Mason (now age eleven). They divorced after Cameron had an affair; he later married a woman, Gabrielle, who had one child (Logan) from a previous relationship. Hailey and Cameron have a contentious co-parenting relationship, in part fueled by her resentment of his affair. Furthermore, both Hailey and Emma are bitter toward Gabrielle for "destroying their home."

The Juan-Hailey Blended Family Map (Figure 1) was created by Blending.Love. We've added relationship "temperatures" that I first discussed in my book *Building Love Together in Blended Families* with co-author Dr. Gary Chapman. Obviously, the details of your Blended Family Map will differ (and the icons used by the website may change with time), but you can still learn about your family from this example.

Family Structure and Ethnic Influences

There are many different stepfamily structures and configurations. Once they are married, Juan and Hailey's family structure will include five adults parenting six children spread over three different homes (Maria's, Juan and Hailey's, and Cameron and Gabrielle's). It also includes many grandparents in multiple households (not pictured here). You can see why I like to say that most blended families are tall and wide—that is, at least three generations tall and multiple households wide.

Juan and Hailey's Blended Family Map reveals the multitude of people and relationships that everyone must manage, not to mention the natural divisions they must overcome to bond and form a family identity. Seeing the reality of your family structure might also be eye-opening and sobering. When picturing the future, engaged couples often see their family as simple. Perhaps you imagine you, your children, and only your household. Former spouses (living or deceased), their new spouses, and the grandparents on their side of the family often don't get included in the imagined family portrait. But the first

Create your Blended Family Map at Blending.Love. Use discount code MAPDEAL30.

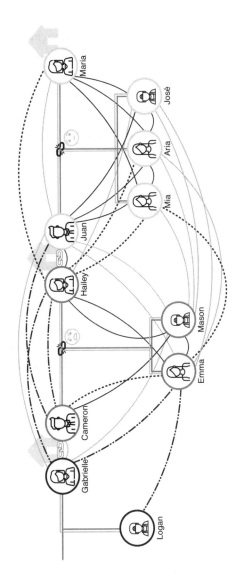

FIGURE 1

Hailey and Juan's Blended Family Map

blending.love
Map Your Blended Family

Relationship with Previous Partner

- Perfect Pals
- Cooperative Colleagues
- Angry Associates
- Fiery Foes
- Dissolved Duos

- Household
- Divorced
- Married
- —— Biological Bonds
- — Legal Bonds

Emotional Relationships

reality you must face is that everyone in your Blended Family Map is going to be part of your family. You might not think of them as being family, but your children or stepchildren do. Seeing the relational connections that exist makes that very apparent. Even former spouses are part of your family from an emotional, psychological, and practical standpoint. They impact your finances, your schedule, the climate of your home, parenting decisions, the well-being of children, the bonding process of new step-relationships, and on and on. Ultimately, everything and everyone is connected. It's important that you accept this so you can be proactive to respond to each dynamic and relationship connected to your home.

Relationship Temperatures

Each two people (called a dyad) have a relationship that could be described in general as "Cold" (awkward or conflicted), "Chilly" (fragile, weak, or in development), "Cool" (friendly or caring), or "Warm and Snug" (strong bond, committed). Of course, relationships evolve and change over time, so whatever label you use describes how you see it today; you might label it something else tomorrow.

Couples often see a few things differently. I encourage you to print two copies of your Blended Family Map so each of you can draw the temperature lines from your point of view. Then share your thoughts and listen to the other's perspective. You're not trying to decide who is correct; you're listening to their perspective (which may reveal their hopes, expectations, and beliefs about each relationship) so you can have a shared understanding of your family dynamics.

Another helpful reflection is examining how different people have differing experiences of the same family. For example, Juan has strong bonds with all three of his biological children and a mutually respectful relationship with his former spouse, Maria. So far, he is developing a friendly relationship with his future stepchildren, Emma and Mason. Hailey also has strong bonds with her two biological children and a friendly relationship with José (future stepson), but things are chilly with Mia and Aria. So while Juan may be feeling very optimistic about the family, Hailey may be apprehensive about her role as stepmom to the girls. Juan may love it when all five kids are together, and Hailey may vacillate between having fun and feeling anxious. It will be important for Juan and Hailey to empathize with each other and understand the other's experience (not take issue with it).

Look at the family structure from the kids' point of view. Because Juan and Maria's co-parenting relationship is cooperative, moving between homes may not be problematic for Mia, Aria, and José. But because animosity and resentment exist in Hailey and Cameron's co-parenting relationship, Emma and Mason will likely have logistical issues moving between homes (e.g., poor communication means things get left behind) and may experience, for example, anger (external behavior problems) or difficulties concentrating at school (internal anxiety issues). That means transition day may be exciting for one group of kids and depressing for another. So how will the parents respond?

And what about the relationship dyads of children—how do they differ? Aria has strong bonds with her mom and dad but is somewhat chilly toward Hailey, with whom she is just beginning a relationship. Emma, on the other hand, has a strong bond with her mother, a chilly relationship with her father, and a cold relationship with her stepmother, Gabrielle. Even though Aria and Emma are only one year apart in age, their emotional worlds are miles apart. How might this impact how each bonds with their new stepparent, or each other? This brings us to the topic of emotional triangles.

35

Relational Triangles and Patterns

Follow the triangle: What Peter tells you about Paul says more about your relationship with Peter than it does his relationship with Paul. It's easy to see that Peter's negative words about Paul reveal he doesn't like Paul, but what's just as important to notice is what his complaints to you about Paul reveal about your relationship with Peter. It might say, for example, that Peter feels safe with you. But it could also be that Peter is trying to form an alliance with you against Paul. Or maybe Peter is just trying to keep you for himself, moving you away from a close friendship with Paul.

And there's more. If Peter is successful in creating an alliance with you against Paul (albeit a surface, pseudo-alliance at best), your relationship will make it less likely that Peter is able to resolve his issues with Paul. Welcoming his gossip, as it were, fosters distance in the other two sides of the triangle. Your relationship with Peter (one side of the triangle) is greatly impacting the other two sides (his relationship with Paul, and your relationship with Paul).

There are numerous emotional triangles on Juan and Hailey's family map. For example, the fact that former spouses Juan and Maria have a respectful, cool relationship makes it more likely that each of their children can have a warm and snug relationship with them as parents. On the other hand, Hailey and Cameron's tense, conflicted, and cold co-parent relationship reinforces Hailey's super-close (we might say *overly* close) relationship with her daughter, Emma, and Emma's chilly relationship with her dad. What happens on one side of the triangle has an impact on the other sides, and vice versa. It doesn't dictate or determine the other sides, but it does influence it. For example, if Hailey and Cameron's relationship improved, it might release Emma to have a closer relationship with her dad—and perhaps even her stepmom, Gabrielle.

Trying to understand emotional triangles can be a bit overwhelming. I'm simply inviting you to look around and make observations—especially as it relates to relationships that seem stuck. For example, in general Juan has a cool relationship with his stepdaughter, Emma. It might help Juan (and Hailey) relax about that developing relationship if Juan can recognize how his conflictual relationship with Cameron and Emma's tense relationship with her dad impact her level of openness to Juan. Juan might understand more why Emma occasionally warms up to him but then backs off when longing for more from her dad. Empathizing with her dilemma can help him be more patient and not take her distance as disrespect. It can also help Hailey not pressure Emma into "going in 100 percent" with Juan. (I'll say more about this in chapter 3.)

Coupleness and Familyness

I invite you to create your own family map at Blending.Love. The questions at the end of this chapter will guide you into making many relationship observations.

Let me remind you that coupleness does not equal familyness.[1] Dating naturally focuses the eyes of most people primarily on their couple (or dyadic) relationship. But becoming a blended family involves so much more. You must now open your eyes to the familyness factors so your coupleness dreams can come true. Said another way, building a strong couple relationship is just part of what it takes to build a strong blended family. Each Growth Activity in this book is meant to strengthen your coupleness *and* move you toward familyness. Don't skip an Activity or leave children out of the ones designed for them; you can't grow familyness without their involvement.

ACTIVITY INSTRUCTIONS

1. Go to Blending.Love and create your Blended Family Map. This will be something you'll refer to throughout the reading of this book. (The Map is very affordable; still, use this discount code to get 30 percent off: MAPDEAL30.)

2. Print two copies of your Blended Family Map. Draw a temperature line or label each dyadic relationship as Cold, Chilly, Cool, or Warm and Snug. Of course, relationship temperatures can change moment to moment. During conflict, for example, your marriage can be Chilly but will return to Warm and Snug after resolving the argument. We're not talking about that. Label each relationship as you see it in general. It's okay (and normal) if you label them differently as a couple.

   • Discuss your labels and perspective. Take turns sharing your Blended Family Maps. Consider the other's point of view and be curious. (For example, say, "Tell me more about that.")

   • Examine the emotional triangles. Pay attention to stuck relationships and the triangles of which they are a part. Discuss how changes in the other two sides might help the "stuck" side.

3. If you think it appropriate, use your Blended Family Map to begin a series of conversations with your children about your journey to become a family. You can even print a fresh copy of the Blended Family Map for each child and ask them to draw relationship temperatures as they see them.

   • Biological parents might choose to have this conversation with their children without the future stepparent present in order to encourage honesty and a candid dialogue. Share what you learn/observe later.

- Listen to your children's perspective on each relationship *before* sharing yours.
- This can be a very insightful dialogue with young and adult children alike.
- Resist the urge to push an acceptance agenda.[2] If your children express concerns, for example, don't try to argue with their logic or feelings in order to get them to accept your new partner or the new family. That may shut them down or make them feel like they are unimportant to you. Just listen and validate that they have questions or concerns.

4. Place Blended Family Maps in a common area of your home (such as on the refrigerator) so they prompt periodic conversations. Developing a common language between family members about the relationships in your home (and future home) is part of defining relationships and co-creating a new family identity.

POST-ACTIVITY QUESTIONS FOR REFLECTION

1. What did this activity open your eyes to? Regarding the process of becoming a family, what do you see more clearly now?

2. What did conversations with your children reveal? What did you learn about their perspective or feelings?

3. Describe your childhood family cultural and ethnic norms. For example, describe gender roles and expectations, social activities, and family celebrations (birthdays, holidays, and special events). Which of those

influences did you carry into any previous relationships (or marriage) and/or still practice today?

4. In light of your Blended Family Map, revisit the circumstances surrounding the end of any previous relationships (death, divorce, or a breakup). But don't just share what happened (the facts). Share the emotional impact it had on you (talk around your pain), any residue still on your heart today, and how the temperature of that relationship is impacting triangles that are forming in your blended family.

5. What did your experiences as a child teach you about the stability of marriage relationships? Share a story that illustrates this.

6. Describe your current co-parent circumstances. How cooperative is your co-parenting? What struggles does this create?

7. A wedding for one of the co-parents often ripples changes into the home of the other parent. (Everything is connected.) What changes do you anticipate in your child's other home when you marry?

8. Consider the temperature of each of your dyadic relationships. What could you do to change the temperature? How might that positively impact those connected to the triangles of which you are a part?

9. OPTIONAL: Share your Blended Family Map and observations with a mentor/pastor/therapist and ask them to help you explore relationship patterns even further.

TRY THIS

Take a stepfamily couple who has been married for a few years to dinner. Tell them what you've learned about your family from this Growth Activity and then ask them to talk about their family structure. Ask them what insights they have gained through the years about their family that they didn't see prior to the wedding and what they wish they had known.

3

HELPFUL EXPECTATIONS

It's helpful if your expectations are based on what is and what will be, not just on what you are dreaming about.

A single man who had never been married was dating a woman with four children by two different men, and two grandchildren. After his pastor helped him draw what would be their Blended Family Map if they married, the pastor said, "Your task in dating is to be sure you can marry this," and he pointed to everything on the paper.

Immediately, the man realized that the happy family he had begun to imagine was based solely on his relationship with his girlfriend; he hadn't fully considered what it meant to marry into a complex family system and be part of a parenting team that included adults in three households. It took staring at the Blended Family Map to realize that.

Maybe your Blended Family Map has begun to recalibrate your expectations as well. This is a good thing because it roots you in what is, not in unrealistic expectations.

If Only It Were So

Let's briefly explore some common unrealistic blended family expectations.[1] Recalibrating your expectations prepares you for what most families experience and puts the two of you on the same page so you can lead from a position of togetherness.

"Family members will love each other right away." If only this were so! It does happen occasionally with some family members, but not with everyone. As it turns out, blended family relationships develop just like other friendships and close relationships: one step at a time, over time. Even when initial connections seem very positive, sometimes there is a "cooling off" once real life begins, then an "up and down, in and out" that continues over time. Sometimes the path to familyness starts with someone keeping another at arm's length. This, too, is normal, so don't be surprised or discouraged. Learn to be okay with one step forward, one step back, until time results in two steps forward, one step back.

One woman wrote to me saying that she and her fiancé were struggling to balance his time every other week with his two children, ages fourteen and twelve, with her feelings of being neglected. The father and his kids would take weekend trips together. He wanted to start including her, but the kids wanted to keep it just the three of them. The woman felt like an outsider and wondered if this would continue into the marriage.

I replied to her with a number of thoughts. "Yes, it probably will. Love takes time to develop, so his desire to include you doesn't mean they will want to include you in the same way. Find points of connection with the kids and slowly work your way in." I also told her something I knew she might not want to hear. I advocate for biological parents spending one-on-one time with their kids before and after a new marriage because it helps reassure children that they haven't completely lost their parent. But a couple hours a week or a weekend getaway every once in a while should be balanced with couple time and family activities that include everyone so the stepmom can build relationships and memories too.

And then I suggested that feeling neglected when he spent time with his kids was her job to manage. Yes, he needed to be sensitive to her and consider her feelings, but he couldn't make her okay. Only she could self-regulate. Expecting him to deter her every insecurity was unrealistic. "Is this revealing some vulnerability in you?" I asked. "Strive to manage your anxiety and not let it get the best of you, or you will grow to resent their connection. Their relationship is not the enemy; your fear is."

"This marriage/family will be better than the last." Don't try to convince your children that this family is better than the first or is somehow "God's plan" for them (which suggests their original family wasn't).[2] And don't think of this marriage as a test to prove, in light of a previous painful relationship, that you really are worth loving. It does make sense that if your first marriage ended in dissolution, you'd want this one to be a stronger, more fulfilling relationship, but don't live comparing everything to the past or you will be, ironically, still married to your past.

"We can merge traditions quickly." By definition, traditions aren't traditions until you've done them enough that people know what to expect and assume they will take place. So your family must wander a little in the wilderness until you figure out what you like and can repeat it enough that people become invested in the tradition. A birthday tradition takes years to develop. A holiday ritual only takes on meaning when it's expected and feels comfortable. And a fun vacation might be preceded by a few failed attempts. Relax your expectations around these experiences and trust that they will take on meaning over time.

"Our kids are invested in our marriage as much as we are." Even when kids love their stepparent and are in favor of their parent's marriage, they often feel a little divided about it as well. They love how their stepparent cares for their parent, but what they really want is for Mom and Dad to be together again. They value what the blended family brings to their life, but a part of them is sad that someone is missing from the family portrait. It cuts both ways. Bitter comes with sweet. Maybe the way to say it is that they just aren't as dedicated to your success as you are. They're not against your marriage necessarily, but they would be okay if you weren't together.

Now, here's what you need to keep in mind: These mixed feelings are the strongest in the early years of your marriage, and they usually subside over time. As the family bonds and they become more invested in what you are creating together, these feelings diminish. What you need to do is love your marriage and give them grace as they learn to love it too.

"My relationship with my children won't have to change." Morgan had two teenage children, and her husband, Aaron, had three daughters ages seven to twelve. Before they married, she saw some things that troubled her but decided they weren't a big deal. For one, he made himself available to his girls whenever they needed him. His attentiveness was admirable in one sense, but it had no boundaries. The reality of this hit on their wedding night when one of the girls called because she couldn't fall asleep without him kissing her good-night, and he suggested they go home and check on her. Did I mention this was their wedding night!

The couple discussed this and other similar actions from Aaron with their relationship coach. It became apparent that Aaron didn't think his relationship with his girls should have to change as a result of his marriage. "My kids didn't choose this," he said. "Just like their mom leaving, they didn't choose this. I did. They still need me."

46

No, actually, your relationship with your children must change. Sometimes fairly significantly. They should not lose you, and you will continue to make marital sacrifices of time, energy, money, and resources in order to care for them. But an abiding commitment to another adult will bring about some change. This does not, however, mean you stop loving your children—far from it. In fact, to embrace your new marriage they need to experience your consistent love, dedication, and presence in their lives. There will be tough decisions about where and with whom, for example, you spend your time, but this isn't a competition. You must choose both your spouse and your children—and invest deeply in each. Both win. Finding the balance in these two investments is not always easy, but working toward it as a marital team will make it more likely.[3]

"Things that trouble me will improve after the wedding." Without realizing it, engaged couples often assume that love will conquer all. You expect those little irritants that you've noticed in their personality to dissipate once real life together begins. The struggles you've had with a former spouse shouldn't affect your marriage much, right? And your fiancé's financial woes will get better once you are managing the money.

Before they married, Jeremiah noticed that Makala treated her two children more like friends than children. And the oldest, Aniyah, she treated more like a co-parent who was helping her raise the younger child. Jeremiah assumed that once he took his place in the home, his wife wouldn't need Aniyah to fill that role anymore. But the relationship was set—and, he would later learn, was part of a generational pattern between mothers and daughters even if a husband was present. Jeremiah found himself surprised that things didn't improve, he was frustrated, and he battled a dynamic that made him "the bad guy" who caused trouble in the family.

Don't assume like Jeremiah that minor or moderate dating irritants will instantly go away after the wedding. Yellow flashing lights send a signal to drivers to slow down and proceed with caution. Ignoring yellow lights or maintaining your speed through a caution zone is ill-advised for safe driving—and for safe preparation to become a blended family. Slow down, take a good hard look, and decide if what you see should alter how you proceed. Keep in mind that some yellow lights turn red.

By the way, because people sometimes assume that love will conquer all, engaged couples have been known to run red lights too. In my book *Dating and the Single Parent*, I review a number of yellow and red lights that dating couples should watch for before deciding to marry. For example, marrying someone who is a poor parent is one of them. Earlier I told you about Morgan, who saw that her fiancé, Aaron, had an overly connected relationship with his daughters (who couldn't go to sleep without him). She assumed it would change after they married. It didn't, and his inability to set boundaries with his girls ruined their wedding night. Jeremiah made the same mistake. Marrying someone means marrying not only their expanded, multi-household family structure; it means marrying their relationship patterns and dynamics, their personality quirks, their credit score, and their spiritual values. If you've been minimizing anything that troubles you, now is the time to name it and slow down before proceeding with caution.

"Blending is the goal of this stepfamily." Much of my writing and teaching career has been spent helping couples realize that you don't cook a stepfamily with a blender. I know some call them "blended families," and ultimately what you likely want is a family that has *merged well* together, but blenders have blades that cut people, their family history and connections, and hopes for the future into pieces. With intense force and Cutco®-like sharpness, blenders force ingredients to lose their identity and merge with other ingredients whether they want to or not. That doesn't create a family that is safe and comfortable for "ingredients." That creates a hostile environment that demands guardedness, caution, and self-protection.

As I detail in my book *The Smart Stepfamily*, the best cooking method to bring family ingredients together is a Crockpot.[4] Gently and persistently, slow cookers, as they are sometimes called, warm up ingredients and soften them so they can with integrity merge their flavor and being with other ingredients. Some ingredients warm up sooner than others; others need more time and warmth before they soften. But each, in its own time, gradually moves toward integration.

It's important that you create an environment of perpetual warmth and safety. Treating one another with respect, expecting people to be kind to others (even if you don't love them), and communicating another's value to you are all good examples of how to do this. But there are others. You could say that my SMART STEPFAMILY SERIES of books (found in the beginning of this book) are all about creating a Crockpot environment to help your family cook. You might complement this book with others that will also aid your cooking process, but understand that you can't rush the amount of time it takes. Like blenders, Instant Pots work fast, but they use pressure to do so. Crockpots work slowly, often taking hours. But that's how you get a good, authentic blend. A quick family integration is attractive, of course, but push too hard and you'll discover things slow down, conflict goes up, and so does stress. Instead, lower your expectations, grow your family slow and steady, and you'll find the taste gets better and better. The average blended family needs years for ingredients to share of themselves and combine (and not all ingredients combine to the same degree; some not at all). Warming, softening, and merging takes time. Embrace that truth with patience and persistence and you'll find more of what you're hoping for.

ACTIVITY INSTRUCTIONS

- This activity consists of guided conversations with each other and your children (and an optional family activity).
- Be honest to identify fears or concerns that arise. Don't avoid being candid. If you identify what might be a yellow or red light, say it out loud to yourself and a friend/mentor/coach.
- During conversations with your children, be sure to communicate your love and continued commitment to them.
- Step into grief. Talking about the future often brings up the loss of the past. Don't avoid this; step into it. Hug any hurt or pain that arises. Strive to let the pain of the past and the hopeful anticipation of the future coexist side by side.

Couple Conversation

1. Do you recognize your own thinking in any of these unrealistic expectations? Share which ones are hard to let go of and why.
   - New family members will love each other immediately.
   - This marriage/family will be better than the last.
   - We can merge traditions quickly.
   - Our kids are invested in our marriage as much as we are.
   - My relationship with my children won't have to change.
   - Things that trouble me will improve after the wedding.
   - Blending is the goal of this stepfamily.

2. Talk through how these expectations have been recalibrated by the chapter. What insights have you gained and how have your expectations been adjusted?

3. Say out loud or write down any concerns that have arisen for you while adjusting your expectations. For example, one person said, "Learning that it will take years to Crockpot our family harmony makes me concerned about my son who is seventeen and about to leave home. What if he doesn't have time to bond like the rest of us?"

4. Consider having some conversations with your children (ages five through adult) about their expectations. See the Parent-Child Conversation section below for a list of suggested questions. Chapter 8 will walk you through discussions about what will likely change after the wedding, but right now you can focus on their hopes and what they think you are expecting from them.

   Don't underestimate the power of these conversations. Not expecting your children to love everyone immediately is one thing; actually letting them talk to you about it is another growth moment for your family altogether. Not discussing these topics potentially puts psychological and emotional distance between you; talking openly about them and empathizing with your children's feelings closes that gap and gives you permission to connect again and again around these subjects over time.

   NOTE: In some cases, it may be best for the biological parent(s) to talk to their children individually or as a sibling group (i.e., without the stepparent); not including the future stepparent or stepsiblings may help children be more candid and open.

Optional Family Crockpot Exercise

Depending on the ages of your children, you might layer the below conversations on top of a fun dinner exercise (first shared in *The Smart Stepfamily*). This is optional. However, I think you might be pleasantly surprised how well children understand and make use over time of this metaphor about your family merging process.

1. Plan a fun Saturday. (This could be a combination of time with everyone together and/or subgroups, like a biological parent and children.) Start the day by gathering everyone in the kitchen. Have a Crockpot recipe ready. Let everyone add one ingredient to the pot. As they do, talk about how your family is like this dish.

   • Note that you are not stirring or blending the ingredients by hand but are relying on the Crockpot to bring everything together slowly over time.

   • Put on the lid and turn on the Crockpot. Wait a few seconds and ask why it hasn't cooked yet. Wait for responses.

   • Point out that for ingredients to merge, they have to warm up, soften, and then share of themselves—and that each ingredient has its own timing.

   • Then point out that the "ingredients" of your family will likely do that too, each in their own time.

   • Talk about how long it takes to cook food in a Crockpot. You might mention that just as it takes a few hours, your family may need a few years to fully merge.

   • Allow people to ask questions.

2. Go about your day as planned.
   - If you get a chance during the day, pause in the kitchen and ask people to observe how the cooking is going.
   - Make some observations (e.g., it's beginning to smell good, but it's not done yet; some ingredients haven't softened as much as others, etc.).

3. At the end of the cooking time, sit down together as a family and enjoy the meal. As you eat, ask what lessons people learned from the Crockpot experience. Pray together at the end of the meal, asking God to give your family patience as you "cook together."

4. Bonus: Incorporate some of the following questions into your day of fun and time together.

Parent-Child Conversation
Modify the following questions based on your child's age and development.

1. It took us a while to get back to normal life after the divorce/parental death. And remember how long it took for you to feel comfortable at your new school/church [identify something recent they can relate to]? How long do you think it will take for us to start feeling like a family after the wedding? Who will have the easiest adjustment? The hardest?

2. What's going to happen to how we do things around the house (like play our favorite game, eat meals, share the bathroom, etc.)?

3. If divorced: I think it's fair to say that you wish your mom/dad and I were back together again, right? Obviously, that's not happening, and I really want to marry

[name]. So, how are we going to do this if you want me to be with mom/dad and I want to be with [name]?

4. If widowed: I know you wish mom/dad were still alive. Me too. Given that, I can see from your point of view how it's weird that I'm marrying [name]. I'm wondering how you can hold a permanent place in your heart for your mom/dad while making room for the relationship with your stepparent?

5. What do you think my expectation is of you regarding [name of fiancé]? I don't expect you to love them like you love me or dad/mom, but do you sometimes think I need you to love them like that?

6. What is your dad/mom's (other biological parent) expectation of you regarding how you get along with [name of fiancé]?

7. What do you think [name of fiancé]'s expectation is of you regarding accepting/loving them?

Follow-Up Couple Conversation

1. Share as a couple what you heard from the children and discuss the implications for your engagement and marriage. If working with a relationship coach or pastor, share these observations with them as well to get their perspective.

2. Finally, review this partial list of yellow and red lights. Which, if any, are even the slightest concern for you? Now is the time to give voice to them so you can begin working together toward their resolution.

   a. Yellow: Do either of you have an oppositional or behaviorally troubled child? (Do you have a sense of

why this has happened? If nothing else, are you prepared to "marry" this dynamic?)

b. Yellow: Do either of you have difficulty trusting the
other? Have past hurts or betrayals left a residue of
distrust on someone's heart?

c. Yellow: Did either of you step quickly into this relationship after a big loss? Less than a year after a divorce or death is generally too quick and just delays
the grief journey till you are married.

d. Yellow: Is pornography a part of either of your lives?
To what degree?

e. Yellow: Are there character issues to deal with? Examples include obsessive-compulsive behavior, a
quick/repeating temper, blaming others for their life
situations, someone who won't respect your sexual
boundaries, excessive debt, excessive enmeshment
or disengagement with their family of origin, decep-
tion/lying, a diagnosed personality disorder.

f. Yellow: Do either of you have a difficult former
spouse or one who has a vastly different moral/
spiritual framework than you? (The values and parenting of the other home will dramatically affect
parenting and relationships within your home.)

g. Yellow: Do you get a sense that your fiancé would
like to change a relationship you have with one or
more of your children? What is their need? Do your
children feel threatened by this?

h. Red: Does either of you feel pressured to marry
quickly?

i. Red: Do you have extreme differences in parenting?

j. Red: Do either of you have a horrible former spouse who spreads contempt and bitterness throughout the family?

k. Red: Has cohabitation drifted into a decision to marry? To establish and maintain a strong commitment, men need the emotional space to freely choose marriage as opposed to waking up one day to discover they slid into marriage.[5]

POST-ACTIVITY QUESTIONS FOR REFLECTION

Many couples cautiously enter the conversations above and come out on the other side with a greater confidence that they are moving, with wisdom and intentionality, in the right direction.

If, on the other hand, the last two activities have raised a check in your spirit, listen to it. Many couples dismiss flashing yellow caution lights, or even red ones, because it means their dream may not be becoming reality as easily or quickly as they hoped. Don't be naïve. Give voice to your concerns and talk through them with a trusted advisor.

TRY THIS

Review the list of titles in the SMART STEPFAMILY SERIES (see the list near the front of this book). Which, if any, jump out at you as something you might want to explore after finishing this book? You might also start listening to my podcast, *FamilyLife Blended* (with Ron Deal), which provides practical guidance on many aspects of stepfamily living. Learn more at FamilyLife .com/blendedpodcast or wherever you get your podcasts.

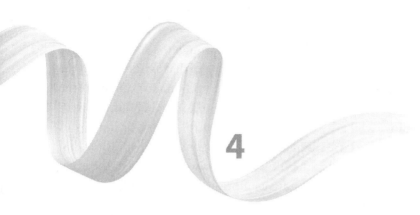

PLANNING YOUR WEDDING

In an early outline of this book, I put this chapter toward the end. But after reading research on the role a well-planned wedding can play in the lives of children, I moved it toward the beginning. Let me explain.

In my book *Building Love Together in Blended Families*, co-authored with Dr. Gary Chapman, I explained that for blended families, a wedding ceremony culminates one process and begins another. Exchanging rings during the ceremony culminates a couple's journey into love and commitment; rings signify permanence. But the ceremony doesn't fully culminate the process of becoming a family. That process begins to a small degree before marriage, but it really expands and deepens for the entire family unit *after* the wedding.

Now, here's the opportunity. The process of planning and preparing for the wedding—and the ceremony itself—can play a part in facilitating family identity and bonding. It can accelerate becoming family to one another.

Have you ever heard about a blended family wedding that ended in disaster because the adult kids didn't show up or one of the children cried all the way through the ceremony? This happens because of the emotional gap that exists between the couple and their children leading up to and throughout the ceremony. The couple is happy and excited about the wedding, while their children are resentful, angry, or hurt by it. Weddings are intended to be moments of celebration that cast a vision for the future, but for some children, the event is empty, full of negative emotion, and a reminder of what has been lost. And for some, the ceremony—because of the way it is structured—actually delegitimizes the marriage. (I'll explain why later.)

But just as a poorly planned wedding can make things worse for your family, a wisely designed experience can improve it. Research confirms that when children are consulted about the decision to marry and the timing of it, when they are actively included in planning the wedding, and they are able to participate in a wedding that lifts high the couple's marital commitment and acknowledges both the children's family of origin and their role in the new stepfamily, they are much more likely to experience the ceremony itself as important and full of meaning.[1] A shared family experience that is positive and rich in meaning—not just for the couple, but for the children as well—contributes to the developing family identity. Though they might not have noticed it while it was happening, people can eventually look back at the wedding and say, "This is when we became a family."

To be clear, wedding planning and the wedding itself don't finalize the process of bonding (that process goes on for years), but they delineate a starting point for the family and can, if managed well, accelerate the process of becoming family.

You really want to get this right.

To that end, let me flesh out the essential elements of wedding planning to avoid and those to include.[2]

The Backstory Matters

What led to your decision to marry, the wedding itself, how events unfolded, and the biological parent's relationship to their children greatly impacts whether they view your wedding—and marriage—as legitimate. For example, a child's relationship with their stepparent initially goes *through* their relationship with their biological parent. As I said in chapter 1, in the beginning, children are most invested in preserving the relationship with their parent; as long as that remains strong, most kids are open to getting to know their stepparent. But a child who for whatever reason feels estranged from their biological parent or replaced by the stepparent in their parent's heart will likely struggle to embrace their parent's new love. A wedding under these circumstances tastes bitter to children. Ideally, a parent in this situation would re-invest in relationships with their children and reconcile before realistically expecting them to open up to the stepparent. (This is why it is so important that dating couples with children attend to the emotional needs of children while at the same time nurturing their new relationship.)

But there are other reasons a child might discount the significance of your ceremony. A parent who quickly remarries after being widowed or divorced, or who recouples multiple times (including serial dating and cohabitation), proving themselves untrustworthy, sacrifices the confidence of their child in their marital decisions. One young man said, "My mom would never let me date the kind of people she dated. I gave up trusting that any of her relationships could last." Or perhaps a child isn't drawn to the person you have chosen. A child who doesn't connect with or like the character of your spouse-to-be can't be excited about how such a relationship will impact you as their parent, them as your child, or the family as a whole.

59

And then there's the complication of grief. A parent's marriage always reminds children of the original loss. Watching Mom commit to love, honor, and cherish a man dramatically calls to mind the fact that Mom and Dad stopped loving, honoring, and cherishing each other. In the case of parental death, planning a wedding resurrects grief over the parent who died and the family unit that perished with them. You can't have one without the other.

Now, while you have some influence over the aforementioned elements of the backstory (e.g., you can attempt to draw closer to an estranged child), the story is what it is. And because of that, you should anticipate how your children might respond to the wedding and wonder what you might do differently at this point to come alongside any confusion or angst they may feel.

The Type of Wedding Matters

Interestingly, some children (especially those in their teens and adults) think a parental wedding should have some elements of a traditional wedding, but not too many. In other words, a big to-do with a white dress symbolizing virginity and "first love" can feel inauthentic and degrade the marriage of the child's biological parents (which the child still cherishes). But the opposite is also true. A civil ceremony doesn't feel traditional enough for some children. It can be criticized as too casual and not serious enough. As one child said, "Well, if you want everyone to take it seriously, it needs to be a little more than a barbeque."[3]

Worthy of note, cohabitation adds to the confusion. What is the role of a wedding when the parent has been living with the other person? *"Were we a family before, or is it just starting now? You're taking your vows now; were you not committed before? What's the difference?"* A casual wedding following cohabitation may not make a strong enough statement about the changing nature of the family. Weddings need to drive a stake in the ground and declare that something, that *everything*, has changed, or they run the risk of being insignificant and not altering the trajectory of the family.

Let the above research inform conversations with your children about the wedding. No, you are not letting your kids dictate what kind of wedding you will have, but in discussing it with them, you affirm their value to you and gain information that will inform your choices.

Involvement and the Elements of the Ceremony Matter

Unless a child is estranged from their parent, most want a fair amount of involvement in both pre-wedding planning and the ceremony itself. They want the messages of the ceremony to honor the past. And they want the wedding to not just be couple-centric, but family-centric. As one young adult indicated in hindsight about her mom's wedding, "I wish it would have helped create a family, not just a marriage."

A second or subsequent wedding for a parent brings three potentially competing emotional attachments into collision with one another: the couple's marriage, the child's loyalty to their family of origin, and the new blended family.[4] We typically think of weddings as being all about the couple (or for that matter, the bride), but a blended family wedding is also about the children, the family relationships that preexist the stepfamily, and the journey everyone has taken to get there. The trick is to acknowledge each of these relationships and not let one completely drown out the other two.

Get wedding officiant content and creative ideas for your wedding at familylife.com/preparingtoblend.

Consider the contrast. A wedding that ignores children, gives them no place in the ceremony, and focuses only on the couple could inadvertently send a strong message to a child that their family of origin is dead, their connection to the biological parent is insignificant, and the new marriage is all that counts. In light of the many losses the children have already experienced, a message like this will for some children strike a deathblow to their hearts regarding the marriage. However, a wedding that includes children in the decision-making, planning, and fulfillment of the ceremony helps children acknowledge the legitimacy of their parent's nuptials and receive the reality of their new family. Balance in celebrating the children's family of origin, inviting them to be part of the newly formed stepfamily, and holding up the new couple's commitment to each other can be a powerful turning point for your family.

Essentially, the three core messages to say to your children in your ceremony are: Our marital "us" matters; your past matters; and your expanding family matters. To overdo any one of those three messages to the neglect of the others could make the ceremony "empty" for a child, but the balance of all three makes it full of meaning and sends the most important message of all to a child: *You matter.*

The elements of a ceremony help send these balanced messages. Exchanging rings speaks to the importance of couple commitment establishing a covenant to last till death do them part. And planning a mother's wedding, for example, around the children's visitation schedule with their dad, and decorating the venue with pictures of the children with their father and extended family communicates an ongoing respect for their past and extended family relationships. And then to help each child see how they fit into the family being formed, the modern Blending of the Sands Ceremony (or a similar ritual) gives them a chance to symbolically pour themselves into what is being created. This doesn't, of course, complete that emotional process, but it does help to jump-start it, especially when children have helped plan that element of the wedding service. Planning helps them envision the moment when they will "give themselves" to the new family, logistical preparation helps them prepare their heart to do so, and participating in the ceremony symbolically marks the day and formally starts the bonding process—which is then walked out in real life following the ceremony.

Taken together, when various elements of the ceremony give all these messages (Our "us" matters; your past matters; your expanding family matters; you matter), children are more apt to legitimize the wedding, the marriage, and the new family in their hearts.

One couple, after reading an early version of this book manuscript, decided not to elope because her children would not witness them taking vows and certainly wouldn't play a part in the ceremony. Instead, Kristin and Jason planned a small but intimate wedding for family and let her children play the roles they wanted to play. Kristin's two boys walked her down the aisle and gave her away (answering the question of who gives this woman to this man with "My brother and I"), and her daughter carried the wedding rings and held her mom's bouquet. Jason added to his marital vows a promise to his new stepchildren to "love, support, and protect" them, and "nurture their growth in the Lord." By the way, in order not to mandate a reciprocal promise, the children were not asked to make any statements back to their new stepfather. However, they did feel comfortable, after the couple's vows and rings were exchanged, participating in creating a piece of family art that would later be placed in their home. Each adult and child painted their hand and pressed their handprint onto a blank canvas. The wedding officiant added meaning to the moment, noting that each of them—in a way they individually decide—now has the opportunity to put their own hand to this family and that each of them will stamp their unique fingerprints to the canvas of what this family is becoming. "And together," he said, "in your own timing and in your own way, you can create something beautiful." (Get more creative wedding ideas like this at familylife.com/preparingtoblend.)

ACTIVITY INSTRUCTIONS

This "activity" starts with a family meeting but might expand from there to a series of individual conversations with children as needed. The cumulative impact of the conversations is a process that includes children in decision-making (adding at least some sense of control to their lives) and lets them contribute to and participate in the wedding in ways that are meaningful to them.

Couple Conversation:

1. If you haven't already, start talking through your wedding and the elements you'd like to include.
2. Try to have a range of options that you are comfortable with—and what you are not open to. Carry this unity with you into your conversations with children.

Initial Family Meeting:

1. Decide who to include in the family meeting. Sometimes it's best to meet with children one-on-one from the start or meet with one group of children, then another. Don't forget younger children; they like to be included and may have more to offer to the conversation than you think.

2. Start by saying something like, "We are excited about getting married. But we also know you might have mixed feelings about it. It's okay if you are worried about how mom/dad might feel about this, or if you feel odd sometimes. We get that and we're not offended. In fact, we want to plan a wedding that celebrates the promise we are making to one another as husband and wife and acknowledges the many people you kids have in your life/family. We invite you to help us do that. So we've called you here to talk with you about the wedding ceremony. We won't get it all decided today, but we can at least hear one another's thoughts."

3. Ask: "Would you prefer a more traditional wedding or something different?"

4. Ask: "There are different elements of weddings these days. What do you think about [name a few you are considering , such as a Blending of the Sands ceremony]?"

5. Reception: "Here's what we're thinking about the reception . . . What do you think?"

6. Close by saying, "As plans for the wedding develop, we may come back to you and ask your opinion. And we'd be honored if you would help with some things. Would that be okay?"

POST-ACTIVITY QUESTIONS FOR REFLECTION

After the family meeting, process what you heard from the kids and move forward with wedding plans. Include them (invite their help and assign duties) when you can. Have additional family discussions or one-on-one conversations as needed.

1. In subsequent discussions, you might acknowledge the bittersweet nature of a wedding for the child.
   - If widowed: "Planning this wedding makes me think about planning my first wedding with your father/mother. I miss him/her. And I know you do too."
   - If divorced: "I realize this wedding means your dad/mom and I will never get back together again. I'm sure that makes a part of you sad."
2. Reflect on the weddings in your extended family. What message did they send and how were they received by you and others in your family? What message will others receive from your wedding?

TRY THIS

Watch some random blended family weddings on YouTube with your children. Ask them how they would feel about various elements of the weddings being in your wedding. You might also watch on YouTube my illustration of the Blending of the Sands Ceremony (search "Sand Ceremony, Blended and Blessed, Ron Deal") and what is really happening on the day of the wedding. Let family members share what they relate to in the video.

CO-CREATING FAMILYNESS

Deciding What to Call Each Other

Have you ever heard someone talk about a stepfamily member in a way that made you feel uncomfortable or worried about how the other person would feel if they heard it?

"This is my mom. And this is her husband."

"She's just my stepmom. My real mom is . . ."

"I don't like my stepsiblings—and I don't want them coming to my birthday party."

On the other hand, have you heard someone speak of others within their blended family in idealistic terms only to find out their family members don't speak of them in that way?

Adult: "I love all the kids the same. There's no 'bonus kids' or 'stepkids' in this household. They're all just 'my kids.'"

Child: "He's my stepdad."

What's Going On?

Language reveals so much. In these examples, the language used comments on the speaker's level of trust and connection—or desired level of connection—to the other individuals. It reveals their perception of the temperature of the relationship (see chapter 2). And it often reveals their needs as it relates to other people connected to the situation.

- A child (adult, teen, or young child) who when introducing their stepdad says, "This is my mom's husband," may be telling you that the temperature of that relationship is at least "cool" and "in development"—and perhaps that they are okay with that.

- From a triangle perspective (see chapter 2), a child's language for their stepparent is always a comment on their relationship with their biological parent of the same sex (e.g., stepdad and dad). The two are inseparable. A child's words about a stepparent might also be influenced by how their siblings feel about the stepparent.

- A parent who says, "There are no stepkids in this house," is telling you what they hope will be the case. They hope for warm and snug temperatures. They hope for healing, trusting, emotionally safe connections between stepfamily members. And in so doing, they reveal the deep-seated hope that preexisting biological relationships will have no bearing on the new step-relationships (something that is impossible).

It's important that you listen for these individual messages and what they reveal. But there's something else.

The difference in language between people also reveals the lack of shared clarity and definition in their relationship. When

68

one person says, "There's no step-relationships in our home," and the other person says, "Oh, yes, there is," it is clear that there is no clarity in the family about who they are to one another or how they relate. "Everyone's the same in this family" may be a hopeful statement meant to bridge whatever gaps exist, but when it collides with language that acknowledges the gaps and declares them okay, conflict, cool temperatures, and entrenched hearts may result.

This gap must be reduced.

Co-Creating Familyness

Biological family relationships have the built-in luxury of non-verbal emotional and psychological connection. A newborn baby doesn't have to speak to their mom in order to be connected. Love just is. Parent-child attachment and identity just is. "You're my son and I'm your dad" doesn't have to be negotiated and decided; it's a given. A mutual, lifelong belonging, dedication, and willingness to care for each other—even if you don't like one another—just is.

Step-relationships don't have that advantage. From the outset they depend on communication. Unless people get to know one another and bring overt understanding to the nature of their relationship, trust will remain tentative and shallow. If they don't co-create shared agreement about the boundaries that will govern their relationship, the expectations they put on each other, the roles they will play in one another's lives, and the moral values that they will abide by, they may never have what we think of as a "family" relationship. Communicating about this takes time and intentional effort. While biological relationships are defined by what is (e.g., "You're my dad no matter what"), step-relationships are defined by what is communicated, negotiated, and co-created. You can't take anything for granted.

How we introduce someone to a third party says a lot about our definition of who they are to us. In addition, the term used to refer to them in everyday life says something about the relationship. For years, people have asked me what the best term is for a stepchild or stepparent to use in referring to the other or to another member of the extended family. Their question assumes there is a correct answer. There is not. It is far more important to their relationship and the developing family identity that people discuss and co-create this understanding. Determining a shared understanding of the terms they will use and why they use them can bring clarity to their ambiguous relationship. A conversation in which each party is heard, validated, and respected, and that results in a shared agreement of the terms of the relationship, moves the individuals toward familyness.

That is the purpose of this Growth Activity.

Terms and the Other Home

As you know from creating your Blended Family Map (chapter 2), some of the relational triangles of your stepfamily connect to people in another home (or to a deceased parent). The terms you negotiate for your home must be filtered through how it will impact relationships with those in the other home.

"Recently my stepdaughter called me 'Mom' for the first time and made a reference to it in her diary," shared Sandra. "Her mother read it last weekend and it created a lot of tension in both homes. My husband's ex-wife called crying and mad. She wants her daughter to call me by my first name only, but I'd prefer she call me 'Stepmom.' My stepdaughter is very much caught in the middle."[1]

I said earlier that a child's language for their stepparent is always a comment on their relationship with their biological parent of the same sex. If the child, for example, feels

70

secure in their relationship with their mother and believes she is comfortable with the child's relationship with the future stepmother, the child will feel more freedom to move emotionally toward the stepmom as soon as they are ready. (Sometimes this includes using terms of endearment for the stepmom.) But if the child is anxious about how their mom will react or perceives their mom to be jealous or in competition with the stepmom, they won't. (With very few exceptions, a child will preserve a biological parent relationship at the cost of the relationship with a stepparent.) Therefore, being aware of this dynamic for a child is critical to any conversation you may have with them. You cannot push them toward a label that makes you feel good but will jeopardize a relationship with a parent in the other home. Rather, they need your permission to respond as they see fit. But most important, they need you to take emotional care of you. Don't ask them to do that with a label.

ACTIVITY INSTRUCTIONS

1. Generally speaking, this is a Growth Activity that can include a future stepparent and stepsiblings. Co-creating something that is acceptable to everyone necessitates that. Having said that, it could be that you decide to include the stepparent but not their children or leave them all out of the initial conversation and have them join a later discussion. Proceed however you think best.

2. Depending on the ages and personalities of your kids, call a family meeting or go on a fun family outing. (You can easily have significant family discussions without the kids realizing it while fishing or hiking! And

side-by-side activity sometimes helps children open up because they don't have to look at you looking at them while they do it.)

3. Open the conversation with something lighthearted to avoid a serious tone.

   • For example, listen to or sing "The Name Game." Also called "The Banana Song," it was written and released by Shirley Ellis in 1964 and is a fun children's sing-along rhyming game that creates variations on a person's name. Have fun singing the names in your family.

   • Turn the corner: "That's a silly song. As we start our family, let's try to figure out what names or terms we're going to use to refer to one another."

4. Use other families you're aware of to make the point that there are many acceptable terms that people can use for stepfamily members. You should also talk around "temperatures" and the triangles kids are a part of so they will be more comfortable discussing these factors as well.

   "I've noticed that your friend Susan calls her step-dad by his first name. And your cousin Terrance calls his stepmom 'Mamma Tanisha.' My co-worker calls her stepmom 'Mom' when they are at home together, but in public she refers to her as 'Candace.' There's a lot of ways for us to do this. We're open to hearing what you would be most comfortable with.

   "But let me say this, we [indicate you're speaking for the couple] want you to know that we don't expect you to use any particular term when referring to us. You are free to use whatever label makes you comfortable as long as we agree to it as well.

72

"We know terms reflect how we feel about each other and that they may change over time. Whatever you feel today is how you feel—and it's okay.

"Plus, we know that you have a lot to worry about when choosing labels—things like whose feelings might get hurt or what another parent or sibling will think. Feel free to be honest with us about this stuff. Also, we know each of you [referring to different children] may have different preferences—that's okay. Just speak for yourself."

5. It's very important at this point for the children to hear the future stepparent say this:

"Please know I respect how important your relationship with your bio mom/dad is and I will never try to replace them. You only have one mom/dad in life; how you use that special term is totally up to you. If anything, I hope to be a bonus parent in your life—but that's my *role*—what you *call me* is up to us to figure out together."

6. NOTE: Children are always reading our nonverbals. If at this point yours communicate that you really aren't open to hearing their thoughts or that you really do wish they would call you Mom/Dad, then you will have defeated the point of the conversation. Check your agenda throughout the discussion.

7. Then ask these questions:[2]

- [The biological parent might ask] "Once we are married, how would you like to be introduced to others by your stepparent? In general, should they say, 'This is my stepson/stepdaughter, or my husband's/wife's son, or something else?' What feels okay and what's weird about this?"

- "In private (e.g., in our home), what term would you like for them to use when talking to you or about you?"
- [The stepparent can now ask] "In public, how would you like to introduce me? When talking about me, what term feels most fitting?"
- "In private, what would you like to call me?"
- "What would you like to call your stepsiblings? Step-grandparents? Other family members?"
- "Now that we've decided this, when do you think these terms might be awkward (e.g., if your other parent is present)? What term would you like to fall back to at that point?"
- "We suspect that for all of us, these decisions will change at some point. Don't hesitate to let us know if you want to make a change. Can you imagine a time when we might start using different terms for one another?"
- "If your dad/mom were here (biological parent living in another home), what part of our decisions tonight would you be comfortable sharing with them? What part would be tough to share?"

8. Once the meeting is over, if you are co-parenting with your kids' other biological parent(s), you have a decision to make: Do you communicate to the parent(s) what you have decided?

   First, it's wise to check in with your child before doing so. How a child responded to the last question of item 7 above may help you decide how to proceed. Their response will also tell you something about what the child is having to do to manage this critical triangle of relationships.

In the best-case scenario, everyone agrees that telling the other home what your home has decided will add even more clarity to the uncertain nature of new stepfamily relationships and between-home relationships. In the worst-case scenario, a child demonstrates great emotional distress or panic over the idea—and it's clear that at this point, you shouldn't communicate what you've discussed. Most people fall somewhere in the middle.

The main objective is not to inform the other biological parent what specific terms will be used. The objective, rather, is to help the other parent understand the process your home went through to co-create language that is mutually agreeable, and for them to know that both the children and they were respected in the process. Learning, for example, that the children were not forced into using any terms brings a sense of peace to the outcome. And imagine a biological mother, for example, learning from her former husband that during the meeting, his fiancée (the stepmom-to-be) told the kids that she will always respect their mother, will protect their relationship with her, and fully expects them to reserve the term "Mom" just for their biological mother. That "no-threat" message has the potential to lower the biological mother's anxiety about the future stepmom because it communicates that the stepmom is not competing with the mother and that she knows the limits of her place in the children's lives.[3]

A sample phone call might sound something like this: "Hey, I just wanted to let you know that we had a conversation the other day while hiking about what terms we will use for one another after the wedding. To honor you, we made sure the kids knew we don't expect them to use the term *Mom/Dad*. In fact, we told them we were comfortable with many different labels depending on the context, and that we just needed to figure it out together. So we talked awhile, and David, Rebecca, and Teague all decided they are going to call my wife by her first name at home, but in public, David and Rebecca will introduce her as their stepmom; Teague, on the other hand, wants to call her his bonus mom.

"I'm telling you this because we know it affects you too. All the kids know I'm talking to you about this so you can speak with them about it if you want. Do you have any questions?"

Keep in mind while doing this Activity that what's more important than the terms negotiated is the co-creation of familyness that is happening in the process. Deciding how to introduce a stepparent to a teacher at school is one practical outcome; communicating openly about the ambiguity in your relationship and learning to trust one another even as you define how you will move forward as family is what you're really after.

Starting your family with intentional conversations around ambiguous and sometimes awkward topics likely means you can have more of them in the future. And with each conversation, you further define—and strengthen—familyness.

Additional Thoughts about Terms: A Rose by Any Other Name

Future stepparent, if a child uses a term of endearment for you sooner than you are prepared for, don't ask them to stop unless you have a significant concern (e.g., the biological parent in the other home will denigrate the child). The biological parent should be the one to ask the child not to. Otherwise, if a child wants to call a stepmother Mom, let them! (Even more, be thankful and enjoy it!) Out of an abundance of caution, some future stepparents have thought it best to reserve that term only for the mother, but a child who feels that drawn to you will likely feel rejected by your refusal. Besides, the whole point of co-creating definition in your relationship is empowering children, not controlling them. Most kids are good at measuring their loyalties and comfort zones. Trust them to do so.

As relationships grow and circumstances change, so will labels. A child who returns from weekend visitation with his father may refrain from calling his stepfather "Dad" for a few days. Leaving his dad heightens the child's sadness and, perhaps, guilt for referring to his stepdad with that special term. After a few days when the sadness wanes, the child may again call the stepfather "Dad" or something similar. Other children may use a term of endearment for a stepparent

---

Permission Denied!

Question: "My ex-husband makes our son feel guilty for calling my husband 'Dad.' How should I respond?"

Answer: I wish that your son were free to decide what label he uses for his stepdad. His father's feelings will surely impact his decision. If your son stops calling his stepdad "Dad," don't make him feel guilty or pressure him to start again. This creates a no-win emotional situation for your son. Further, your husband should strive not to take this personally. This isn't about him.

Some kids find a way around this, for example, by only using the term "Dad" when his biological father is not around. Tell him, "I know you are in a tight spot between your dad and your stepfather. Please know that whatever name you want to use is okay with us. The real joy here is you, not the labels."

(e.g., "Mamma Sara") unless the biological parent is physically present. Changing the label protects the biological parent's feelings.

A child's age can also be a factor in the name game. Very young children tend to use loving terms like "Daddy" and "Mommy" very quickly, but then may back away from them once they get older. The label change is often indicative of the child's greater sensitivity to loyalty issues or emotional changes in the relational triangle.

Please understand that the labels your children use are not crucial to your family's success. Co-creating relationship definition and bringing clarity to your ambiguity is what moves you toward becoming family. Labels are just labels. Love in the heart is what counts. A rose by any other name is still a rose.[4]

POST-ACTIVITY QUESTIONS FOR REFLECTION

After the family meeting, talk as a couple about what you heard from the kids. Have additional family discussions or one-on-one conversations as needed. In subsequent discussions you might explore how it has felt so far putting your decisions into practice by asking questions like these:

- "The other day I called you my stepson again. I know we decided that was okay, but now that I'm doing it, how does that feel?"
- "Are you having any second thoughts about what we decided last week? Is there a term or phrase that feels weird to say?"
- "Have you thought of something else we didn't talk about?"

1. Now that you know how to have a conversation defining labels, have the same conversation with your parents, extended family, and friends when you can. They are probably unsure whether to refer to you as a stepparent or bonus parent too, and themselves as stepgrandparent or "Pa Pa."

2. Should you call yourself a blended family or a stepfamily? Does it matter? Learn how this question parallels the focus of this chapter at www.smartstepfamilies .com/talking-blended.

3. Read more about how labels impact the loyalty conflicts children experience at www.smartstepfamilies.com /caught-in-the-middle.

PARENTING TOGETHER

All parenting teams disagree from time to time. Biological parents in first marriages disagree, and so do parent-stepparent couples and co-parents in blended families. Sometimes they fiercely disagree until they find a way to work through it. Whether the issue centers around an adult child who needs support, a teenager and their smartphone, or how you will divide responsibilities for the care of a newborn, disagreement is to be expected. But when parent and stepparent disagreement results in ongoing gridlock, conflict, and isolation, two predictable things happen: the marriage suffers and the family slows—sometimes stops—merging.

I wish I were overstating this, but nearly three decades of experience and research tells me I'm not. Occasionally a couple will ask if they can have two different parenting styles in one household. "We've each been raising our kids very differently and they're used to that. Can't we just continue parenting as we have?" "You can," I reply, "but your family will remain relationally separate—outsiders will remain outsiders—and there may be power games, kids caught in the middle, and resentment in your home."

If that's not what you want, you must take this chapter and your journey toward unity in parenting seriously. To be divided in parenting is to keep your family divided.

I've been making this point for decades, and still most couples ignore it; before marriage, they don't proactively work toward a common approach to parenting and don't plan for how the stepparent's role will differ from the biological parent's role. In our book *The Smart Stepfamily Marriage*, David Olson and I report on our study of couples creating stepfamilies. Taken in 2006, this is still the largest survey ever conducted of couples forming stepfamilies (with some follow-up analysis as well). Our book reports on what best predicts distressed and healthy stepcouple relationships and how you can strengthen your blended family marriage. (Consider it a great follow-up read after finishing this book.) As it relates to this chapter, we found that 41 percent of what contributes to a husband's satisfaction level in the marriage and close to half (46 percent) of the wife's satisfaction is strongly correlated to stepfamily adjustment and parenting issues. We also found that parenting matters cause increasing marital conflict over time unless the couple is working from a posture of unity.[1] And yet, the average couple doesn't spend focused time discussing these topics. Only about half of premarital stepcouples discuss issues related to child rearing as they prepare to form a stepfamily.[2]

This doesn't serve your future well. Some couples think talking about potentially divisive topics will slow their progress toward marriage. Some naïvely assume, as I discussed in chapter 3, that love will conquer all. Neither is true. David Olson and I found that compared to struggling stepcouples, happy couples were 1.5 times more likely before marriage to have discussed and agreed on how they will parent together after the wedding, nearly twice as likely to have agreed on how they will discipline their children, and twice as likely to have negotiated their religious expectations for the home.[3] Not having these conversations leaves your relationship vulnerable.

Now, let me close by saying this: If your parenting discussions result in some changes, don't make all the changes at once. If you do, your kids may experience expectation whiplash and behavioral confusion. Carefully talk through changes that will result in more unity and work into them slowly, one step at a time.

A Vision for Healthy Parenting in Blended Families

A complete guide for good parenting is beyond the scope of this book. I have written two specific books about this topic that I would recommend to you. *The Smart Stepmom* and *The Smart Stepdad* are written for stepparents and have chapters for biological parents to help you with the details of parenting and co-parenting in a blended family. In addition, my book *The Smart Stepfamily* and the revised and updated edition of my video series *The Smart Stepfamily DVD* (now available for streaming online) provide a comprehensive examination of every aspect of stepfamily living, including multiple layers of parenting and co-parenting, in order to equip you for the long journey. (I also contributed to another parenting resource that is worth watching, FamilyLife's *Art of Parenting* video series.) But I can lay out for you here, in brief, a vision of what is involved in smart stepfamily parenting. Like a syllabus for a college course, the below key aspects of parenting represent topics of study that will enrich your family journey. The Activity in this chapter will then invite you to step into a few of them as you begin to negotiate how you will parent together. If you get stuck, I suggest you consult one of the previously mentioned resources for a more thorough examination of parenting in a stepfamily.

Learn about good parenting.

Knowing principles of good parenting is a must. There is a multitude of books, resources, and courses available to help you learn the basics of raising children. Every parent needs a toolbox full of parenting skills, tools, and strategies to draw on as they walk with children over time. You also need to learn about yourself, what triggers reactivity in you, and how you can cope with it. Our love for our children and desire that they experience good things in life makes us vulnerable to their immature decisions and actions. Emotional dysregulation when a child rebels, for example, results in parents tossing their own parenting philosophy out the window, overreacting, resorting to shaming tactics to control a child, and a multitude of other coping strategies that hinder the parent-child relationship and train children to walk in shame and fear. Knowing how to emotionally regulate yourself—that is, having self-control—is one of your most important tools in parenting.

Learn about good parenting in blended families.

Most, if not all, resources on good parenting assume a parenting system comprised of two biological parents. Be careful in how you apply them. Blended families, when you include all the parenting authorities from each home, have multiple people and multiple intersecting dynamics that these resources do not address or take into consideration. Before you can apply their parenting advice, you must lace in an understanding of stepfamily realities.

You will learn about some of these underlying dynamics in the section that follows, but let me give you one example. Many good biological parents find becoming a stepparent confusing and exasperating. The relational equity that they held with their own children isn't a given in their developing relationship with stepchildren, so their ability to guide, influence, and punish is frustrated. Add to that the dynamic forces of living in the shadow of a deceased parent or having a biological parent in the other home undercut their position in the family, and stepparents can feel powerless very quickly. An ambiguous role in a child's life does not allow parents to implement the good parenting advice found in many books (remember, most parenting advice is meant for parents in a two-parent biological family). What is needed is an understanding of stepparent-child bonding, how stepparents evolve their relationship with stepchildren over time, loyalty conflicts in children, stepfamily development, and the role of the biological parent (spouse) in creating an environment of respect for stepparents (discussed in part below).

Study good co-parenting across households.

Have you ever wondered what it would be like to be the ambassador from the United States to one of our arch enemies? The hostile, sometimes war-infused nature of the countries' interaction would make negotiation and mutual respect difficult, if not near impossible. Well, if you are a co-parent and have an angry, embittered relationship with your child's other home, you are in just that position.

Co-parenting has the goal of working with the adults of your child's other home in order to raise the child well. If the climate of your co-parent relationship is generally cooperative, you will find that goal much easier to accomplish. If it is fiery, unworkable, or unreliable, you will not. Commit yourself to learning as much as you can about effective co-parenting and to gaining skills that will aid your between-home cooperation. Here are a few guidelines from my book *The Smart Stepfamily: 7 Steps to a Healthy Family*.[4]

1. *Work hard to respect the other parent and his or her household.* Agree that each parent has a right to privacy, and do not intrude in his or her life. Do not demean the other's living circumstances, activities, dates, or decisions, and give up the need to control your ex's parenting style.

2. Schedule a regular (weekly to monthly) "business" meeting to discuss co-parenting matters. You can address schedules, academic reports, behavioral training, and spiritual development. If you cannot talk with your ex face-to-face due to conflict, use instant messaging, email, or text. Do what you can to make your meetings productive for the children.

3. Never ask your children to be spies or tattletales on the other home. This places them in a loyalty bind that brings great emotional distress. Celebrate the positive relationships they have with those in their other home.

4. When children have confusing or angry feelings toward your ex, don't capitalize on their hurt and berate the other parent. Listen and help them explore their feelings without trying to sway their opinions with your own. If you can't make positive statements about the other parent, strive for neutral ones.

5. Children should have everything they need in each home. Don't make them bring basic necessities back and forth. Special items, like a specific shirt or a smartphone, can move back and forth as needed.

6. Try to release your hostility toward the other parent so that the children can't take advantage of your hard feelings. Manipulation is much easier when former spouses harbor resentment toward each other.

7. Do not disappoint your children with broken promises or by being unreliable. Do what you say, keep your visitation schedule as agreed, and stay active in their lives.

8. Make your custody structure work for your children even if you don't like the details of the arrangement. Update the other when changes need to be made to the visitation schedule. Also, inform the other parent of any change in job, living arrangements, etc., that may require an adjustment by the children.

9. Help children adjust when going to the other home:
   • If the children will go on vacation while in the other home, find out what's on the agenda. You can help your kids pack special items and needed clothing.
   • Provide the other home with information regarding your child's changes. A switch in preferences (regarding music, clothes, hairstyles, foods, etc.) or physical, cognitive, or emotional developments can be significant. Let the other home know what is different before the child arrives.
   • When receiving children, give them time to unpack, relax, and settle in. Try not to overwhelm them at first with plans, rules, or even special treatment. Let them work their way in at their own pace.

10. If you and your ex cannot resolve a problem, agree to problem-solving through mediation rather than litigation.

Teamwork

Let's turn our attention to how you will parent in your home. All good parenting involves teamwork. In blended families, the biological parent and stepparent must work hard to find their harmony, to support one another, and to play to one another's strengths. As you prepare to blend, here are five keys to becoming a good team.

Key 1: Biological Parents Must Be the Parent

Before championing the stepparent's role, the biological parent must first function consistently in the role of primary parent. Hopefully you are doing this now, because you have to continue doing so after the wedding, especially around matters of nurturance, affection, and punishment. Until the stepparent has had time to develop a bond with the kids and earn respect as an authority, you need to clearly be the authority. Look at it from your kids' perspective: You are the safest, most well-defined parent figure in their life. Be that parent.

Here's the problem for those of you who haven't been *that parent*. Making the change to become the primary nurturer and manager of their behavior may be met with resentment from your kids and a blaming of the stepparent even though it isn't their doing. Let's say, for example, that during the single-parent years, you lowered your behavioral expectations, and your children got used to not obeying. Raising your expectations now will likely result in some conflict in your new family. Nevertheless, you need to do what you must to become *that parent* because you have the leadership authority to raise the standard (the stepparent does not). Find the courage to lead.[5]

Key 2: Biological Parents Must Pass Authority to Stepparents

One challenge to stepparenting is developing a relationship with a stepchild that affords the stepparent the needed authority to follow through with rules and impose consequences for disobedience.[6] Until such a relationship is built and trust between stepparent and child established, how does a stepparent function as a parental authority? They must live on borrowed power from the biological parent.[7]

Parents pass authority to the stepparent when they make it clear to their children that the stepparent is an extension of their authority. Saying something like, "I know he is not your dad, but when I am not here, he will be enforcing the household rules he and I have agreed on. I expect you to be courteous and respect him as you would any authority figure," communicates your expectations clearly. Be sure to then back up the stepparent just like you would a baby-sitter or your child's teacher at school.

Key 3: Biological Parents Should Build Trust in Stepparents

One of the greatest barriers to entrusting your children to your spouse is a fundamental lack of trust in the stepparent's intentions. In a two-parent biological home, couples don't seem to question the motives of their spouse. They may not agree with the specific parenting decisions of their spouse, but they don't question their spouse's love or commitment to the child. Parents generally assume the best about the other biological parent's motives. Stepparents are not always granted that same benefit of the doubt.

Zachary loved his wife, Brianna, very much, but he just wasn't sure why she was critical of his two daughters. Brianna complained that Zachary was too easy on them and she feared they would grow up to be "spoiled, boy-chasing girls." Zachary believed that Brianna's real problem was jealousy; he interpreted her criticism of the girls as her attempt to step between Zachary and his daughters. Therefore, he ignored her input and discounted her efforts at discipline.

In order to give your spouse the benefit of the doubt, you must force yourself to trust their motives. Sometimes stepparents *are* jealous, but that doesn't mean they are mean-spirited toward your children. If you don't strive for trust, you'll continually defend your children, even when ill-advised. Your children will learn that obeying the stepparent is optional (since you'll stick up for your children), and your spouse will truly grow to resent your children. Open yourself to the stepparent's input and trust her heart. Talk, listen, and negotiate.

Zachary and Brianna's story illustrates another point. It is very common the world over, says stepfamily expert Patricia Papernow, for stepparents like Brianna to want more limits and boundaries with their stepchildren and for biological parents like Zachary to lean toward understanding and mercy for their children.[8] This is as natural as grandparents wanting to—and feeling the right to—spoil their grandchildren. Each parent must find their way toward the middle. It doesn't help things when parents label the other as *permissive* or *strict*; that just creates defensiveness in the other and closes your mind to their perspective. Consider the other's point of view and resist the temptation to polarize toward the opposite end of the love/limits spectrum.

Key 4: Stepparents Should Move into Relationship and Discipline Gradually

Since authority is based on relationship and trust with the child, stepparents should move gradually into relationship first, then discipline. Good parenting, you may have read, involves a balance of love and warmth on one hand and firm boundaries and correction on the other (what is generally referred to as "authoritative" parenting). To start your family off well, it is crucial that the biological parent reflect both ends of this continuum and the stepparent focus almost exclusively on warmth and relationship building. (Some stepparents will need to remain on this end of the continuum indefinitely.) To be more specific, it is very important that limits and boundary setting come from the biological parent.

Researcher James Bray says one of the most important step-parenting skills is *monitoring the children's activities.*[9] The focus of monitoring is strengthening the relationship with the child. It involves knowing their daily routines, where the children are, who they are with, and what extracurricular activities they are involved in, but does not necessarily include being involved in the child's emotional life. It is parenting that is sensitive to the pace of the child, not pushing too hard for closeness, but continually being an active presence in the child's life in order to allow for relationship to grow. Monitoring stepparents check homework and daily chores and befriend stepchildren yet refrain from emotional closeness that is unwelcome to the child. Bottom line: Good stepparents listen to the child's level of openness, and they keep trying to nurture a relationship with their stepchildren, even if they are rejected again and again. They are persistent and gracious. And in the end, much of the time, a connection is created that is beneficial to the child, the stepparent, and the marriage.

Once a stronger bond is built between stepparent and stepchild, a natural authority to teach, train, and discipline begins to grow. There are two kinds of authority: positional authority and relational authority. Positional authority is what your boss at work has over you, and it's what a teacher has in the classroom. Their position in that context gives them authority. Relational authority is much more influential—and difficult to obtain—because it is based on trust. Caring about your boss's evaluation because you're hoping for a raise is one thing; caring about her opinion because as friends you have come to respect her is another.

Stepparents come into the stepfamily with positional authority. That is, because they are an adult, they are afforded some authority as is any adult, teacher, or neighbor. When children come to care about the stepparent as a person and value their relationship with them, then a stepparent has gained relational authority. Initially, positional authority is dependent upon the biological parent's backing; relational authority stands on its own. Obviously, relational authority is an attractive goal for stepparents, but it must be earned the old-fashioned way—you have to earn it by nurturing a relationship with the child. A stepparent who walks into a family claiming the rights of relational authority without having earned them frequently finds resistance from children (or at least one child) and resentment from their spouse for being heavy-handed.

A child's trust, respect, and honor grow out of a relational history with a stepparent that comes with time and positive experiences. Successful stepparents are dedicated to relationship building over the long haul and don't try to force their way into the child's heart. They also understand the limitations of positional authority in the first few years of the stepfamily and rely heavily on the biological parent to manage the children until their own relational influence grows.[10]

Helen called to complain about her husband's parenting of her son. "Larry's not abusive, but he will always say no to whatever Brandon asks, and when he walks in the room, Larry tells him to do chores or some task. He doesn't make conversation with Brandon, relax, or open up to him. I feel like I am always running defense for my son, and it is the biggest cause of fights in our marriage." Larry was critical and nonaccepting of his stepson, and it was pushing both his stepson and wife further away. Larry needed to learn ways of connecting with his stepson. Lightening up, being humble and willing to engage Brandon in his interests, sharing his own talents and skills with Brandon, complimenting him, and showing appreciation for how he contributes to the home are just a few ideas he could implement.[11]

Key 5: Align Your Parenting Strategies

I started the chapter by saying you cannot have two vastly different parenting strategies in your home. Aligning your parenting is a significant aspect of your family merger. By the way, if your children are adults, this principle still applies. No, you aren't directly responsible for their behavior, but you are still influencing and mentoring them, and the boundaries and expectations around emotional closeness and your involvement in their lives are still being played out every day. All these aspects of parenting need to be brought in alignment with adult children too.

I've decided there are many good ways to parent children. Good parenting tactics are one element of parenting, but what matters just as much (or more) is that you decide together how you will parent. Unity is vital. As was said earlier, reading good books on parenting and discussing the principles will help move you toward a common parenting posture. You can also watch other parents and learn from them, invite an older couple with a solid track record to mentor you, or attend formal classes on the subject. Over time I suggest you do all of the above, but you might as well start now.

The following Activity is designed to start you on the journey of finding unity. Don't rush through it. Let each part surface what needs to be discussed. Your goal is to co-create a plan for how you will move forward *together* as parents. This is not your definitive plan for all time! It's just a starting point. Beginning to walk out your plan will inevitably bring about revisions. Let life teach you what you need to change. Just get started. Can you begin to implement some of your strategies now, even before the wedding? Yes, absolutely. Test it out, knowing that what you discover will inform and help revise how you move forward after the wedding (when life gets very real for everyone).

ACTIVITY INSTRUCTIONS

Use the following questions to learn more about your current parenting practices and each other's ideal parenting philosophy while co-creating a plan of how you will parent together. You will not be able to work through these questions in one sitting; rather, pace yourself with a series of conversations. Some questions will open big topics that may last awhile. If you are talking with a mentor or pastor on a regular schedule, discuss as many as you can between meetings, then, if needed, continue your parenting dialogue even after moving on to subsequent chapters.

1. If you are a biological parent, what's one aspect of your parenting that you're working on and why?

2. Say out loud or write in just a few sentences your basic philosophy of parenting as it relates to each of these subtopics (consider the developmental ages of your children):

   a. Teaching spiritual values and beliefs

   b. Expressing love to a child

   c. Motivating children toward responsibility

   d. Punishment for misbehavior

   e. Being friends with your children versus being an authority figure

3. How did your parent(s) handle these aspects when you were growing up? How is your style similar or different from theirs and why?

   Discussing how you were parented as a child is important. We know that most people get their practical parent training from how they were parented. Couples who were parented similarly find it easier to come together around their parenting philosophy and practices. In our research, 82 percent of all couples acknowledge they were parented differently by their parents as a child, but those who were parented similarly were 11.5 times more likely to have higher quality couple relationships.[12] So explore your history openly. Being parented differently as children likely means you will need to be very intentional to bring your stepfamily practices in line. Also, as you explore these questions, go back to your Blended Family Map (chapter 2) and indicate how each parent (stepparent, grandparent, and any authority figure in your childhood) parented you and your siblings. Tell each other two sets of stories: Ones that symbolize the everyday parenting you received (and how you felt about it) and stories about the extreme moments you experienced. This last group of stories might be difficult to tell, but include them, as they often leave a residue of either joy or pain on our hearts.

4. Review the following descriptions of parenting styles.[13] Which best describes your childhood parents/authorities? Which best describes your parenting style over the past few years? If you have a co-parent, which best describes their parenting style? Again, it might be helpful to record these labels on your Blended Family Map for easy future reference. You can also note how children respond(ed) to that form of parenting; this may help you notice patterns between homes and across generations.

   a. Democratic Parenting. Sometimes referred to as authoritative, these parents establish clear rules and expectations and discuss them with the child. Although they acknowledge the child's perspective, they use both reason and power to enforce their standards. They balance being emotionally connected with their child (having solid, loving relationships) and being flexible (providing structure, clear expectations, and limits). When behavioral lines are crossed, children are firmly admonished, but love remains. This combination of emotional warmth and boundaries brings out the best in children. (A quick note: as discussed above, initially in a blended family the biological parent should be the one setting boundaries and enforcing consequences when boundaries are violated.)

b. Authoritarian Parenting. These parents have more rigid rules and expectations and strictly enforce them. They expect and demand obedience from their children. The authoritarian style is characterized by very structured parenting while closeness and loyalty to the family are highly demanded. (A quick note: In general, authoritarian parenting by stepparents in the first few years is toxic to stepparent-stepchild relationships and should be avoided.)

c. Permissive Parenting. These parents let the child's preferences take priority over their ideals, and rarely force the child to conform to reasonable behavioral standards. Expectations and rules are chaotic at times and easily manipulated because these parents prefer to keep the peace with their children. A warm, affectionate friendship with the children is the parent's most important priority.

d. Rejecting Parenting. These parents do not pay much attention to their child's emotional needs but have high expectations regarding how the child should behave. These families have little emotional connection; children are not sure they are loved due to the parents' disengaged style. An environment with high expectations and little emotional support creates children who feel they aren't good enough; failure comes with great insecurity and shows itself in low self-esteem, immaturity, and a variety of psychological problems.

   e. Uninvolved Parenting. Also called neglectful parenting, these parents often ignore children, letting the child's preferences prevail as long as they do not interfere with the parents' activities. Like the rejecting parent, uninvolved parents are emotionally disengaged, but they don't have rigid rules or expectations. Rather, they are overly flexible in their structure, leaving the child alone without consistent boundaries.

5. Which of these forms of correction have you/would you utilize? How frequently? Give an example. If there is a co-parent, which do they frequently utilize? NOTE: Just because a strategy is listed does not mean it is a recommended form of correction.

   a. Explaining or talking to a child about their misbehavior and how it affects others

   b. Spanking, slapping, or swatting (corporal punishment)

   c. Discussing right and wrong/appealing to the heart

   d. Yelling

   e. Criticizing the child

   f. Ignoring misbehavior

   g. Reviewing rules and codes of conduct

   h. Demeaning or shaming the child

i. Lecture

j. Making the child feel guilty

k. Coaching (e.g., helping a child apologize to a sibling or decide how to cope with a friend in need)

l. Counting to give them time to correct behavior

m. Time-out

n. Giving extra chores

o. Taking away objects (e.g., toys) or privileges (e.g., going to bed without a meal or taking the car keys)

p. Withholding love or yourself from the child

q. Natural consequences (e.g., if a child forgets their lunch they go without)

r. Logical consequences (e.g., if you spill your milk, you clean it up)

s. Rewarding improved behavior

t. Other: What additional strategies do you/might you utilize?

6. Discuss why it's important to "catch kids doing something right," that is, pay attention to good or respectful behavior and applaud it. How often should this strategy be utilized, in your opinion?[14]

7. On a scale of 1–10, how good are you at:

a. Managing your anger toward a child, especially when feeling disrespected or ignored?

b. Following through on what you said you would do?

c. Looking for improved behavior?

d. Helping children know what is expected?

e. Listening to your child when they feel a rule is unfair or something needs to change?

    f. Separating a child's behavior from your identity? For example, not feeling personally embarrassed by poor or unwise behavior?

    g. Not being manipulated by guilt trips or a child's sadness?

    h. Encouraging a child, building them up?

8. On a scale of 1–10, how well would your children say you remain self-controlled and calm when they misbehave? What do you need to improve to emotionally regulate yourself better in these moments?

9. In general, would you rather tell a child what to do or help them make a decision for themselves? Explain why.

10. What are your boundaries around money and the use of family assets? How and when do you share money with children?

11. What responsibilities do you expect children to have as they grow (e.g., chores)? How should they contribute to the home and the family?

12. What are your ideal behavioral boundaries and expectations for smartphones, the internet, social media, and screen entertainment?

13. Hot topics: What current behavioral matters are you concerned about? What can you anticipate in the months/years ahead?

14. Discuss these common mistakes of biological parents and stepparents. Which have you made already? Which might you be vulnerable to make in the future?

    a. Common Biological Parent Mistakes

      • During the single-parent years, becoming soft with expectations and/or not following through with discipline.

- Refusing to do the hard things of parenting (e.g., taking the lead in punishment or telling a child no). This creates a gap in the home that stepparents try to fill before they have enough relational equity, which usually increases family conflict and sabotages the stepparent.
- Not trusting the stepparent's heart for the children.
- Not making space in parenting decisions to include the new stepparent (leaving them out).
- Becoming easily defensive or dismissive when the stepparent makes suggestions or questions a parenting decision or pattern.
- Allowing past pain and hurt with a former spouse to sabotage your co-parenting cooperation.
- Going behind the stepparent and undermining their involvement.

b. Common Stepparent Mistakes

- Acting like you're trying to replace their biological mom/dad (whether living in another home or deceased).
- Expecting children to embrace you without hesitation.
- Not making fun a priority.
- Expecting children to immediately accept the stepparent's authority at the same level as a biological parent. Not growing into your role.
- Taking a child's hesitation to accept you as rejection (it's often just confusion about where to put you in their heart).

- Making unilateral decisions without the biological parent's agreement.
- Expecting to make right the "wrongs" that exist in the biological parent or the routines/patterns of the household (e.g., changing foods or birthday traditions to suit your preferences).
- Being harsh, temperamental, or cold with stepchildren.
- Not allowing the children to spend time occasionally with their parent (your spouse) without you. In the beginning, children need reassurance they still have access to their parent and some things will remain the same.
- Speaking poorly of the child's other household in front of them.

15. If your children move between homes, what co-parent dynamics/patterns are you currently facing?

   a. Which movie title best describes your current co-parenting relationship (e.g., *Die Hard*, *Jaws*, *Singin' in the Rain*, or something else)?

   b. What are the parenting rules or values of the other home that stand in contrast to yours, and how do you cope with them?

   c. To what degree do your children get caught in the middle of conflict between homes?

   d. What leftover hurts interfere with cooperative co-parenting?

   e. Future stepparent: What observations or questions do you have about your fiancé's co-parenting situation?

POST-ACTIVITY QUESTIONS FOR REFLECTION

1. Based on your discussion so far, say or write a few sentences about what you've learned about how you will parent together. What is your plan? What needs to change and who needs to own the change?

2. Begin to implement some of what you've discussed (even before the wedding). Children should be told *by the biological parent* about significant changes before they begin.

TRY THIS

- Listen to episodes of my FamilyLife Blended podcast addressing stepparenting, co-parenting, between-home transitions, and navigating the holidays, and discuss the key principles you hear. Use these podcasts over time as a catalyst to conversations that move you toward oneness in parenting.

- For more strategic ideas for bonding emotionally with stepchildren, read my book *Building Love Together in Blended Families: The 5 Love Languages and Becoming Stepfamily Smart,* co-authored with Dr. Gary Chapman (Northfield Publishing, 2020), and take the Love Languages Profiles, modified for blended families, in the book.

7

CREATING A SHARED GRIEF JOURNEY

Your wedding is about your family's future. So why do we need to step back into the losses of the past? In most chapters to this point, we've been thinking forward as we examined relational expectations, planning the wedding, introductions and bringing definition to family relationships, and parenting together. But it's time to reflect again on your Blended Family Map (created in chapter 2) and take note of who has a place in your family story but is not living in your home. Blended Family Maps create a present-day snapshot of an intergenerational family narrative, but you cannot fully understand the present without tying it to the past. Said another way, you and your children must occasionally step back into the past so you can understand it and, in some cases, grieve it, because it is always a part of your present and future.

People on your Blended Family Map who are absent from your home today (e.g., a parent) represent a plot line of your family story that is carried into the present. Their map icon symbolizes positive memories and emotions like love, comfort, belonging, stability, trust, and peace, as well as hard realities like conflict, hurt, betrayal, cancer, anger, uncertainty, pain, tragedy, financial distress, and broken dreams. That one little icon represents every joy and longing, comfort and pain—and everything that led up to their departure and what has happened since. Likewise, the addition of new people to the Blended Family Map again points back to the original loss (i.e., what happened that made their presence possible) and brings new losses and transitions to the family in the present (e.g., changes in family roles and routines, parenting, living conditions, social network, etc.). I find that many stepfamily adults want to run from this reality. For example, they want to pretend that a deceased parent will not impact the role of a stepparent in the home or that a fiancé's former spouse's values and lifestyle will not affect parenting decisions in the new blended family home. Not true. You cannot avoid these realities, nor should you. To attempt to blend your families without acknowledging loss or the presence of the past is to remain blind and disconnected from one another. You cannot truly love one another and ignore this elephant in the room.

My goal in this chapter is to foster both individual and family grieving. You will not complete it—you never finish grieving significant losses—but you can grieve forward, *together*. Even more, family grieving not only helps individuals reposition the past and carry it with them in healthy ways, but it fosters emotional bonding between new stepfamily members.

Each person has their distinctive individual grief journey. Most of us seem to be aware of that. But far less recognized is a family's grief journey. For example, a biological parent and their children have a collective journey following a death or divorce. It may come in the form of conversations around what has changed, what it means, and how they are going to cope. It may come in the form of hugs and shared tears. It may come in the form of mutual indignation and frustration with God and each other. And it may require shifts in chores or responsibilities around the house, economic adjustments, new ways of caring for each other, and different living conditions.

Some families do this well. Others have never grieved together at all, only separately. They grieve in isolation from one another. Whichever the case, I want to help you and your children grieve with more intentionality—and now add others to the collective grief dialogue, namely stepparents, so children experience them as caring, compassionate friends with whom they are emotionally safe.

Just consider the alternative. When a stepparent lacks sympathy for a child's sadness, it may harden the child's heart toward the stepparent. Without saying a word, a stepparent's coldness communicates messages like, "Your dad is dead; I'm your new dad now," or "Aren't you over this yet? Your loss isn't a big deal," all of which thicken a child's loyalty to the person or reality they are grieving (e.g., a deceased parent or the idea of their parents still together) and increase their rejection of the stepparent. Stepping on a child's grief is for some stepparents a mortal sin from which they never recover, but the opposite is also true. A stepparent who compassionately enters a child's grief, gives permission to it, and by their willingness to grieve with the child, sends the message, "You should grieve your father; I respect that and will help you," or, "I understand you grieving that your parents aren't together anymore; I can give you space to wrestle with that." Besides helping the child, this has the added benefit of fostering bonding between stepparents and children and furthering the "cooking" process of the entire family unit. When new people and old ones become safe harbors for one another, respect develops and familyness deepens.

Earthquakes and Aftershocks

I know a lot about grief and family grieving. Unfortunately, I've been there and am doing that. In February of 2009, my wife, Nan, and I went to see the movie *Taken*. The movie is about a father whose daughter is abducted—that is, taken—for sex trafficking. After the movie, we returned home to find our middle son, Connor, complaining of a headache. Little did we know that at that very hour, Connor was being taken. A MRSA staph infection had contaminated his body and was systematically destroying his lungs. Over the next ten days we rode the roller coaster of hope and fear until finally descending into the valley of the shadow of death. Connor was gone from this life. Taken.

There is no recovery from this. There is only surviving and trusting God for enough grace to get through (which he has graciously provided). For Nan, me, and our other two sons, life is forever changed.*

At first after a monumental loss like this, life stops. Completely. You are in a fog, a daze of disbelief and overwhelming sorrow. You can't imagine going on. For what? How? Why? I didn't seem to care about anything. Everything was trivial at that point and our grief was all-consuming. Questions filled my mind. *What do I do with this hole in my heart? How do I love my wife and other boys? How do we grieve together? We have different emotions, intensities, needs to talk or be silent, questions, and perspectives on what happened and God's place in the situation.*

And then life forces you to start living again, but you don't know how. I had to go back to work. Our boys had to return to school. We still had responsibilities that wouldn't go away;

---

*Hear Ron and Nan recount their story of loss, grief, and their journey to find grace on this podcast: www.familylife.com/podcast/series/connors-song.

birthdays, holidays, and anniversaries we couldn't celebrate; and spiritual rituals that seemed powerless and lifeless. As life moves ahead, the questions persist. *Where was God? Where is he now? What good is prayer? How do I love my family when I don't care about anything? How do I parent when I'm so distracted? How do I cope with the varied reactions from others—some of whom are angels of mercy and others just plain stupid and without compassion. And how do I be around people who are shallow and hollow in their perspective about life—people with "normal" complaints that I, too, once had, but now I find petty and ridiculous?* Questions, questions, questions. Pain, pain, pain. It's inescapable and completely overwhelming.

Loss of this magnitude is not a onetime event. It starts with the original earthquake and is then followed by a series of ongoing aftershocks that add to the destruction. Aftershocks that may continue for years and years—or a lifetime.

I think you, too, have had a similar journey. Yes, the specifics of your grief journey are different, but maybe you and your kids can relate to the process. First came the death, divorce, or breakup, and then come the aftershocks:

- A lost sense of self, identity, and struggles with your self-worth.
- Fun family rituals, like a pizza and movies on Friday nights, become hollow, empty reminders of what was but isn't anymore.
- A loss of social belonging: Friends or family members who won't engage you as they did before or church members who treat you differently.
- Feeling helpless to help your children wrestle with their grief and the realities of what is happening.

107

- Worrying that your kids will doubt God, when you yourself doubt him.
- Financial struggles.
- Changes in parenting, values between homes, and not knowing how to respond.

This list likely goes on and on. Without much effort you can probably list five to ten aftershocks that you're dealing with right now. Yes, in many ways, the impact of the original earthquake has subsided in intensity and you've gotten back to life, but the residue of dust still coats your heart and relationships.

Just a few minutes before writing this, my wife and I had a phone call with our oldest son, Braden. He is twenty-six and has COVID-19. We've known this for a few days, but now his throat is hurting badly and he's wondering what he can do about it. He's tried over-the-counter medicines with little relief. He called the Teledoc (because the clinic won't let him enter), but they couldn't prescribe anything stronger. Should he go to the ER? Another doctor said he should avoid that unless his breathing is labored. Too many questions and not enough answers. Bottom line: This is triggering a lot of fear in my wife and me. We've been down this road before, and we can't help but be fearful of what could happen. Others might brush this off and say, "Oh, he's young and healthy. Odds are he'll be fine." But you can't say that to us. Life has already taught us—with severe permanence—that what we think will never happen to us, can happen to us.

And it's taught *you* that unfortunate lesson as well.

The best of intentions don't always produce the outcome you desire. Tragic stories are not just about others; hurt is something that happens to you. You can't unlearn this. But you—and we—can strive to put your trust in God, manage your fear (so it doesn't manage you), and share your anxiety with others around you so together you can share the load.

Here's the point: Tragic and terrible loss requires intentional grieving. The trajectory of your life is forever changed (dare I point out that you wouldn't be getting married if something tragic hadn't happened), and you must be proactive with each other and your children to cope with it or you will fall prey to grief's heavy weight. Grief is an emotion that will not be denied. For a moment you can pretend it doesn't exist or isn't relevant, but you cannot erase its presence.

After twelve years, Nan and I can tell you that our grief is far less intense and debilitating than it was the first several years. We can smile again. Laugh again. And release ourselves to enjoy life. But our sadness is not gone. There are moments when it rushes back on us like a massive ocean hurricane wave. And triggers, like another son's illness, bring it all back and fill us with fear. (By the way, our oldest son recovered from COVID and we are grateful to God for it.)

Do not ignore grief. It is unkind to those who grieve. View it, instead, as a companion in your family's journey. An unwanted companion, most certainly, but one you must pay attention to.

Family Grieving Starts with You

I'm wondering what the last section has resurrected in you. Has it reminded you of your grief (past or present)? Do you feel it in your body (head, neck, or back pain, stomach tightness)? Did you find yourself restless as you read that section? Take notice, right now, of what is rising up in you. It is telling you something about your grief, and your response is telling you something about your typical coping method. Do you talk about it? Are you swallowing your feelings? Are you feeling sad, angry, helpless, bitter, confused? Listen to yourself.

If you have never been through great suffering but are marrying someone who has (and their kids), you may not be feeling much of anything. Or maybe you are aware that you can't really relate to their pain. That is important to be conscious of because it can inadvertently translate into a lack of compassion for their sadness and minimizing their pain. Not only will that result in your being unable to grieve with those who grieve, but it will put an emotional gap between you and them that could be offensive or make you unsafe, someone to avoid and hide from rather than someone with whom they can trust their inner emotions. It's important that you can come alongside their grief.

I'll say more about that in the section that follows, but for now, let me emphasize that good family grieving starts with the adults in the home. Whether you are the biological parent or stepparent, you have a role to play. During the Growth Activity, you will discuss the following strategies.

Grieve out loud. Make sure you talk openly about your sadness. This communicates that it's okay to grieve, be angry, not know how to feel, and have concerns. Sometimes parents want to convey strength and inadvertently communicate that sorrow is off limits. Children and teens need to know how to think about loss. When you go first, you show them how to grieve and give them permission to do the same. Don't confuse talking about your sadness with making your children your emotional caretakers. While not putting the burden of your well-being on their shoulders, talking openly about your grief essentially says, "We're in this together," and invites children to lean on you with their sadness.

Connect faith and life. When you communicate your grief through the lens of faith and moral values, you help children see how faith and life connect at an important level. This matures children as you grieve together. First, it teaches that vulnerability and "not knowing" is a part of life and does not equal weakness. And second, it shows children how to think through a situation from a faith-informed, value-centered perspective. Grief is innately self-centered. Infusing it with a spiritual perspective informs pain with that which helps us transcend it.

Listen, affirm, and validate . . . don't try to fix. To do this means being able to endure the child's pain because you cannot fix their pain; you can only hug it. A small child who falls and skins their knee will most assuredly cry out in pain. You can put a little medicine and a bandage on the abrasion, but mostly what they need is a hug. A little TLC somehow helps the hurt. It doesn't fix the skinned knee, but somehow the child feels better. This is the way you help children of every age with the scrapes on their hearts. Time and again you pull them into your lap, letting them cry over what hurts. Wrap listening with compassion and, when you can, physical touch. Somehow it helps.

Practice emotional coaching. One compassionate way to respond in those moments is with emotional coaching. In his excellent book *Raising an Emotionally Intelligent Child*, Dr. John Gottman says that parents should teach children to recognize how their emotions are impacting them and how to self-regulate their behavior despite their emotions. He outlines several steps to emotion coaching.[1] Begin by being aware of your own emotions and what you are feeling in the moment. Managing yourself appropriately models what you are teaching the child to do.

Next, seek out the key emotions in what the child is saying, and label them. Small children in particular often don't have a vocabulary for their emotions. They know how to act mad, but they don't recognize the sadness beneath. You will have to point that out to them so they can connect their experience with the emotion ("I can tell you are really angry and perhaps a little sad right now. Do you know what you are sad about?"). This is important because it gets to the heart of the matter. Focusing only on the above-the-surface issue won't help them deal with below-the-surface grief.

After labeling the emotion, remember to resist the temptation to fix it. "Don't feel bad. Everything will be okay." "Your dad doesn't mean to hurt you." These attempts to fix sorrow won't work. Even worse, they minimize the child's pain and shut them down. The message is, "Stop feeling and talking about this." We want just the opposite: for them to talk more about this—and share it with you. You must find a way to endure a child's sadness or you will never really hear it—and you won't be able to help them walk through it.

By the way, why do we say such things? Because we are uncomfortable with their pain and want to relieve them of it. I'm sure you want to stop seeing them suffer. Perhaps you feel guilty or somehow responsible. Whatever the reason, wanting to make a child's sadness go away is, of course, understandable, but trying to make it go away only distances you from their heart. What goes away is you, not the pain. Don't try to fix it.

Finally, while labeling the emotion is a good first step, try to, in effect, open the wound to hear more. Consider this example of a child who returns home after a weekend at his mom's house. Ten-year-old Brennan walks in the door snippy and curt. Not his usual self, he speaks to his stepmom, Carmen, with a disrespectful tone. In the past, Carmen has interpreted such behavior as rejection. She would snap back at Brennan and the two would bicker until she sent him to his room "until his father gets home." This time, she calmed down and focused in on his experience.

Brennan: [in a harsh, disrespectful tone] "Do I still have to do my chores tonight? I already did some at my mom's

house. It's not fair!" [Stepparents make easy targets
for the frustrations children feel; try to remember that
much of what is directed at you is not about you.]

Carmen: [in a calm tone; she momentarily sidesteps the disrespect and begins to label the emotions she hears] "Hold
on a second. I can tell you are really irritated about having to do chores twice. Am I getting that right?"

Brennan: [his response baits Carmen to take the issue
personally] "Yes. Your son only has to do chores in one
house, and I have to do them at my mom's house and
here. It's not fair."

Carmen: [she skirts the lure and stays centered on Brennan's emotion, wondering what's behind it] "You're
feeling put upon because you have to do chores twice.
I can see how you might feel that way. [That last part
disarms Brennan a little; he's not used to her empathizing and not taking the bait.] I'm also wondering if you
are angry you had to leave your mom's house and come
home. It's hard to do that, isn't it?"

Brennan: [now refocused on what is painful] "I guess so."

Carmen: [digs a little deeper] "It hurts when you enjoy
being with your mom and then have to leave. I can see
why you might come home a little grumpy and sad."

Brennan: [calming down] "It's not fair that I have to leave;
I only get three days there and Mom cries when I leave.
I hate that."

Carmen: [now realizes how deep his sadness is; replies
softly and gently with compassion] "I'm sorry. That
really stinks for you. I know your mom loves you very
much and you love her. It's very hard coming back to
our house. [There's no attempt to fix his emotions, just
acknowledgment. She pauses . . .] Could I give you a

hug—or do you need a little more time first?" [TLC at its best. She gives him a verbal hug just by saying she wants to physically hug him. She also gives him permission not to hug her if he can't do so comfortably right now.]

Brennan: [showing how torn he is] "I'm not quite ready yet."

Carmen: "Okay. I'll hug you later when it feels okay for you."

[At this point, Carmen has earned the right to address the initial disrespect that started the exchange. Her emotional coaching has refocused Brennan and proved herself safe for him. Connection before correction increases her authority. She continues calmly . . .]

"You know, a little while ago you spoke harshly to me. I know you came home feeling cruddy, but I don't deserve to be spoken to that way. I don't appreciate it and don't want you to do it again. Next time, if you come home feeling yucky, I'd rather you walk in and tell me that so I know to give you some space until you feel better. That way we won't argue. Could you do that?" [Waits for response.] "I forgive you, but I'd still appreciate an apology." [Waits for a response.]

[smiling big] "I'm still going to give you that hug later. You can go now."[2]

It might be that this exchange will help Brennan to better manage his emotions and disrespect and the two of them just might have started down a different path together. Notice how they got there: Carmen managed her fear of rejection, shifted away from her own emotions to Brennan's, helped label his emotions for him, validated that he had reason to feel that way, and pursued connection with his emotions before correcting

114

his misbehavior. By coaching Brennan through the moment, she prevented grief from putting distance in their relationship and instead turned the moment into an opportunity for shared grieving. Now catch this: What made all of this possible was Carmen's self-control.

At some point, if Brennan can't stop being disrespectful when he's sad, Carmen and her husband may need to impose a consequence for his behavior. Either way, the emotional coaching should continue.

Stepparents, don't erase and replace. Send a message that you are not competing with the object of the child's grief, but respect and honor it. In the previous case study, Carmen affirmed how hard it was for Brennan to leave his mother. This not only validated his sadness, but communicated that Carmen was not trying to replace his mother. It's very important that children understand this about you so they don't toughen their resolve to make sure you don't.

Step into a child's grief at strategic moments. Because we carry grief with us through time, look for opportunities for family grieving. When a song triggers a memory in yourself or a child, reflect on it. Tell a story related to the song and what it reminds you of. Or when a picture, meal, movie, or circumstance calls attention to what has been lost, acknowledge it. Special days (e.g., birthdays, religious rituals, anniversaries) and holidays predictably trigger sadness because of who isn't present or a tradition that can no longer be kept. Anticipate this and plan how you might comment on the elephant in the room.

Before their father died, Eric's stepchildren spent every Labor Day weekend four-wheeling with their father. They'd fish, camp, and go on long walks together. Even before he married their mother, as Labor Day approached, Eric asked the kids to show him pictures and smartphone videos of their time together. Not all the kids wanted to share their memories, but most would. He

115

laughed at their stories. He shared his sadness that they could not make more together. And when Labor Day actually came, he didn't try to replicate the scenario. Instead, after talking it through with their mother, he made it possible for her and them to go to their paternal grandparent's house for the weekend . . . without him. Giving them time to be with that side of the family—and not inserting himself into the weekend—was a huge blessing for everyone.

Other thoughts to keep in mind:

- If your child doesn't seem to be grieving, keep monitoring. Children grieve in spurts. Just because you don't see it doesn't mean the pain won't resurface later. Plus, they could be hiding their feelings to relieve you of the burden of worrying about them. Children who don't cry worry me the most. Remain open to the possibility that future life circumstances may release emotions that have been hibernating, and continue sharing your feelings so the child will know it's safe to talk when the day finally comes.

- Some young children will express their feelings best through art or play, which allows them to tell us about their pain without having to use words. Finding a qualified art or play therapist can be very helpful.[3]

ACTIVITY INSTRUCTIONS

1. Before talking with children, discuss the following as a couple: If you have been through a significant loss, describe your initial earthquake and then list a few past and current aftershocks that you experience and/or see in your children.

2. Revisit your Blended Family Map and make a list of each family member and the losses you believe he or she has experienced. You might print off a new copy of the Blended Family Map and write the losses beside each person's name. Imagine what it has been like to be that person at each point along the way: before the breakup/ divorce or death of a parent, after the divorce/death, during the single-parent years, and after your engagement was announced. Finally, anticipate what each may experience after the wedding. Share this list with your fiancé. (Seeing this accumulated list of losses may help you recognize how much each person has been through.)

3. Now, make a list of grief triggers that resurrect these losses for each person. Triggers can be anything—sights, words, smells, songs, places—that tap into sadness and resurrect feelings of grief, anger, resentment, pain, depression, or other strong emotions. Triggers can change over time, so try to capture the most recent that you've noticed in yourself and others.

4. As a couple, discuss the grieving strategies listed above in the "Family Grieving Starts with You" section. Which are you doing well at this point and which need some attention?

5. Ignite conversations with your children about loss, some one-on-one and some as a group. It's best not to call a family meeting in order to foster family grieving, but to take advantage of the symbols and situations of life that naturally tap into grief. A casual bike ride with your kids can be an opportunity to remember how their deceased mother taught them to ride. A movie or dinner out can be symbolic of a previous time the family spent together. Use these moments to ignite

conversations and nudge hard emotions to the surface. When children do express themselves, stay curious (e.g., "tell me more about what makes you sad about that").

6. If you haven't done so already, have a family conversation that sets the boundaries for how you will talk about feelings of sadness going forward. Your goal is to let each person share when and how it is best for them to be involved in grief conversations (e.g., one-on-one, before special days, during, or after). Because they are uncomfortable with grief, someone may say, "never," so make sure you also communicate that this will be something you bring up from time to time even if they don't want to go there. Hearing what is helpful to each person helps you respect their needs to the degree you can.

7. If a parent died, make a trip to the cemetery with whoever wants to go. Ask kids if they are okay with the future stepparent going—and if not, respect their wishes.

8. Start conversations with statements/questions that get below the surface.

   a. "My guess is you will feel two very different things at the wedding. Happy for me and sad that your dad/mom and I are not together anymore. Can you see yourself feeling that way?"

   b. If you were widowed: "I got to thinking about something the other day. As excited as I am to marry Jane/John, it makes me miss your mother/father. I miss the way she/he would . . . Has my engagement made you miss them too?"

   c. If you are divorced: "I know our divorce has put you through a lot, and I grieve what cannot be for you. I was thinking, if I were you, I'd be a little sad that . . . (e.g., you're going to have to get used to a stepmom/

118

dad/stepsiblings in the house). Or maybe you're feeling hurt or angry that I'm getting married because . . . (e.g., this means your mother/father and I can't get back together). Or maybe you are worried how this will impact your mom/dad. Is any of that on your mind?"

d. "What's difficult for you to get used to as you think about the wedding, my marriage, and our new family?"[4]

POST-ACTIVITY QUESTIONS FOR REFLECTION

1. Revisit the list of losses you made for each family member in item 2 above. After talking with the kids, what else can you add to their list?

2. Discuss the implications for parenting and stepparenting your children based on their accumulated losses. What might you do differently and what will you keep the same?

3. Knowing that guilt and sadness for what children (of every age) have experienced can result in permissive parenting, how can you guard against this?

TRY THIS

- Review the expanded section on loss, grief, and menacing emotions in *The Smart Stepfamily: 7 Steps to a Healthy Family*, chapter 9. It reviews common losses for both adults and children after death, divorce, or the dissolution of cohabiting households.

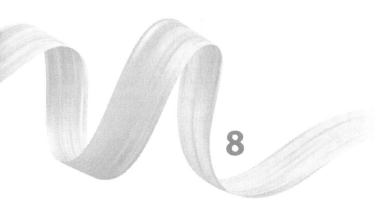

8

ANTICIPATING WHAT WILL CHANGE

Standing in a large, empty tank and having six inches of water added will not cause alarm to the average person. You get wet, but you don't feel anxious. But it would make you anxious if you were already up to your eyeballs in water. What feel like small changes to adults can feel overwhelming to children who are already nearly drowning in a sea of unwanted changes. You can't always lessen the amount of water coming in around them, but you can hold their hand and tell them they aren't treading water alone. The ultimate purpose of this Growth Activity is to acknowledge with children that more change is coming and to communicate, "You're not alone in this. We are with you. Let's find our way through." By the way, there are times when adults need to try to lessen—or stop—additional water being added to a child's tank. Signs of distress in your children may be a signal that their tank is filling too fast or making it hard for them to breathe. For example, you may not think you're rushing to the altar, but your kids might. And changing homes, schools, churches, social circles, and making it more difficult to get to their other parent may not seem like much to you, but it can be overwhelming to them. If they are "drowning," your family is going to struggle. Monitor each child's tank; if your child is struggling to cope with the water pouring in, do something to slow it down. For example, the biological parent might spend a little more one-on-one time with their child(ren) and ease off time when everyone is together. Your presence will reassure the child that they are not alone in their tank.

A secondary purpose of this Growth Activity is to draw kids into the logistics of forming a stepfamily and help your family learn to problem solve together. Inevitably, there will be practical and relational changes that will occur when you blend two families. This activity will help you put them into perspective and discover how you will manage them together. You may want to talk through some of these items individually with children, teens, or adults, but talking through them as a group shows everyone the value of family meetings—a helpful strategy you may continue periodically or regularly. Giving children a voice in decisions helps them to feel valued, teaches responsibility and critical thinking skills, and helps your family take on a team spirit. In some cases, group decisions will provide long-lasting, workable solutions to matters; in other cases, the decision will be just the beginning of a live-and-learn process. Feel free to revisit and adjust decisions over time as the family learns what really works best.

Learn more about Family Meetings at SmartStepfamilies.com /family-meetings.

Discussing changes—and clarifying what they mean and don't mean—also helps you keep logistical changes from inadvertently negatively impacting relationships. Sometimes children, when insecure because of the many changes going on around them, equate logistical shifts to mean there has been a relational change. An adult child may wonder if changes to your will reflect a shift in your commitment to your grandchildren. Or a younger child may think, "Mom doesn't pick me up from school anymore and we don't get that car time to talk like we used to, so I guess I'm not as important to her." Despite being inaccurate, this conclusion will have significant negative psychological impact on a child. This Activity provides a chance, for example, to explain why it will be more convenient from now on for someone else to pick the child up and to reassure the child that they are just as loved as ever. By the way, in a case like this, try to replace some of the lost one-on-one time however you can. As I explained in the introduction of this book, during times of stress and transition, kids need more exclusive time with their biological parent, not less.

The following is not a comprehensive list of changes that may occur when a blended family is formed, but it will focus your thoughts and help you see them from a child's point of view. Please add other areas to your discussions as you think of them. When it comes time to discuss them as a family unit, start with what you think is most pressing, and feel free to spread them out over multiple conversations.

A Seismic Shift

In chapter 7 I described loss as a series of earthquakes and aftershocks. Because single-parent families often reorient themselves around the parent-child relationship, your marriage is yet another earthquake to your children. Committing yourself to your spouse "till death do us part" at your wedding is a seismic shift to the emotional climate of your home. Of course, this does not mean you stop loving or caring for your children, but there is a new significant relationship in your life that will be reflected in your dedication to each other and how you spend your time and energy. Do not hear me say that you must choose one over the other; you are choosing both your spouse and your children. But the marriage will change how some things get done and how time is spent. Acknowledging this while at the same time reassuring children of your continued love and dedication to them will be part of the Activity.

Let's drill down on this a little further. This also activates the emotional triangle that impacts child(ren), parent, and stepparent, and it can feel like another six inches of water to a child who is already struggling to keep their head above the waters of loss. It's critical that you gain empathy for each person in the triangle.

Let's begin with the children. After the wedding, when a child witnesses their parent relationally turning toward the stepparent, it often feels as if the parent is turning away from them. (I've repeated this a few times throughout the book because it's important that you receive this truth.) This change might activate nervousness ("Did I just get replaced?"), competition ("I'd better position myself between my parent and stepparent"), and anxious pursuit of the parent ("Complaints, anger, sadness, depression, or whiney behavior might draw my parent back to me"). Why would this happen? Because the child is manipulative or controlling? No, because six inches of water just got added to the tank. They want, and need, to feel reassured of their parent's love and presence during this change.

It's important to note here that some engaged couples begin to feel this tension before a wedding (especially if they're living together), but others may not feel it in a significant way until after the wedding when they merge family households. Until then, many dating couples are able to naturally compartmentalize their developing couple relationship from the children. Until everyone moves in together, children don't have to face on a regular basis moments when their parent turns toward the stepparent and away from them. But once you live under the same roof, this change becomes obvious, and their "insider" status with their parent becomes challenged by the "outsider" stepparent.

This is also when stepparents—the second party in the triangle to consider—feel the temperature of their relationship with the children growing cooler. They seemed to warm up to you before the wedding but now are cooling off. This emotional whiplash is confusing unless you recognize what has changed for the children and the emotional work it requires of them to keep their heads above water.

The biological parent—the third part of the triangle—is generally trying desperately to remain close to both their child(ren) and their new spouse. And given "cooler temperatures," the biological parent often feels caught in the middle. To turn toward one party is to turn away from the other. Not really, of course; you still love the other. But you are aware that the other is unsure of your love, which makes you feel stuck and at times guilty for every choice you make with your time or energy.[1]

It's important that you recognize that this insider-outsider push-pull dynamic is unavoidable; it is inherent to the nature of how blended families are "born." Some of you enter the Crockpot as insiders (biological family), and some don't. One way to mitigate this dynamic (I don't think you can prevent it) is to begin talking about it even before it happens—and then calmly continue to talk about it once it kicks in. This chapter's Growing Activity is designed to get that conversation started and helps each of you turn toward one another. Putting words on the experience of children helps them feel cared for and creates awareness of what they are feeling. Having empathy and respect for what others in the emotional triangle are experiencing during each conversation will help you validate and connect to one another because those qualities make it easier to adapt to the unwanted relational changes that are occurring. A stepparent, for example, might compassionately say to a child, "I imagine it's hard for you when your mom sits by me instead of you when we're watching a movie. How does that feel to you?" Or a parent might say to both the stepparent and their children at the same time, "I know this is hard, but I love all of you. When I spend time with the other, I'm not saying I've stopped loving you. It's just the other's turn. I hope you can hold on to that."

Here's one last tip to help you manage this triangular push-pull: carve up the triangle on occasion. Yes, your entire family needs to spend time together developing connections and building memories, but it is crucial that couples spend time alone. *And,* as I shared earlier, it's vital that a parent spends one-on-one time with their children. Whole family time is what adults often want after the wedding; make sure you are just as, if not more, intentional about the individual relationships. Don't over-orchestrate familyness, or it may become harder to find.

Daily Routines and Time Together

As your wedding approaches, you may have already changed some daily routines. Although many couples begin to integrate their lives well before the wedding occurs, officially merging your households and every aspect of your lives will likely change your schedules and daily routines significantly.

Walking through your day with kids to explore how having new people in the house will change breakfast, chores, getting to and from school or work, etc., will help everyone begin to think through the logistics and get used to the idea that such changes are coming. Routines, as well as cherished rituals and traditions, help to tell us who we are and give definition to relationships. Your new life may require that routines change, but try not to lose the meaning or connection the old routine offered. Having breakfast together each morning and talking about the day ahead, for example, is more than just a routine. For a single-parent family, it gives everyone focused time together before the day begins and schedules take everyone in opposite directions. It also gives a parent a regular opportunity to affirm each child. Having that routine changed by the presence of a stepparent and stepsiblings not only dilutes their planning time for the day, but it steals the regular dose of nurture the biological parent gets to share with their child(ren). When routines like this need to change, strive to find another way to share meaningful connection, or children may feel that six inches of water has just been added to the tank.

Rituals, Traditions, Holidays, and Special Days

As with routines, holiday traditions, annual activities, religious rituals, and how you celebrate birthdays make statements about family identity and belonging. So in general, try to change as few as possible in order to retain the value behind the ritual or tradition, but when a change is needed, talk it through.

Negotiating that change is not easy. For example, when it comes to combining traditions, be flexible and keep something old, make something new, and borrow from each other till you find something that works. He and his kids open Christmas gifts on Christmas Eve. She and her kids open them Christmas morning. You might try to pull something from each tradition forward while you figure out what will work long-term. To start, you might open gifts both Christmas Eve and the next morning, but run it by the kids first so they can speak into the changes.

Remember—and this is important—there's no one right answer. What works the first year may need to change the next, and what works for you may be entirely different for another blended family. Be considerate, talk through the options, and maintain a live-and-learn attitude.

Primary Residence and Physical Space in the Home

"I used to have my own room. Now I have to share. And she's a pain and there's not that much closet space!" Just like married couples have to learn to share a bathroom, family members have to learn to share the Wi-Fi, TVs, screens, toys, furniture, and yes, the bathrooms. They also have more people to compete with to sit in Mom's lap, and someone else is sitting in their designated chair at dinner. Every one of these changes has the potential to be annoying and to affect how someone sees themselves and their place in the family.

Some couples merge into one person's household; others move out of both and buy a new home. There are many necessary considerations and good options. Changing living situations can be welcomed or unwelcomed by children. Help them anticipate the change and what it will mean for them.

Faith Perspectives

Increasingly, blended family couples come from differing religious backgrounds. They may be more similar than different (e.g., two different Christian denominations) or more different than similar (e.g., totally different faiths with deep cultural rituals attached to them). In either case, there is need for a family discussion about what will change. By the way, in this area I encourage you as a couple to determine the direction you will lead your family in before talking to them. They need to see your conviction and unity.

School

Changing schools is a significant adjustment for kids, especially older children and teens. It means making new friends and losing old ones, finding their place, forming new routines, and adapting to new educational expectations. This should not be a short conversation. Spend ample time helping children prepare for the change.

Social Life

The older children are, the more invested they are in their social connections. Unless there is good reason for change, this is one aspect of a child's life that I would encourage you not to touch, especially for teens and young adults. Having stability in their friendships can help mitigate the other changes going on in their home.

Visitation Schedule and Logistics

Here's another area of their life that should not change unless it simply cannot be avoided. Significant changes in access to the other parent will make accepting and enjoying the new family more difficult. Children of every age need consistent contact with their biological parents. Do what you can to preserve that. If you move farther away from the other parent, then you should carry the burden of making sure contact continues.

Other topics include, for example, how things will change when part-time children visit the home or who will be responsible for certain chores based on who is physically present. Adult stepfamilies may need to discuss how time with the grandparents will be divided and who will host Thanksgiving. Adult children who are married have in-laws to consider, so this can get complicated quickly. Try to plan early, make sacrifices, and be flexible.

Vacation

As with traditions, family members sometimes have definite ideas of what vacations should entail. You'll need to discuss differing preferences and negotiate where you will go, how the time is spent, and what it will cost. By the way, some families find that retaining some meaningful getaways for the biological parent and children while creating new traditions for the entire stepfamily affirms established relationships and builds the new ones. It may take you a few years to figure all this out, but agreement in this area may contribute memories that positively impact family harmony.

Money and Spending Habits

How financial decisions are made, attitudes about spending, and how money is shared with children are elements that might change after your wedding. Helping children anticipate these changes eliminates surprises and gives you an opportunity to teach them about wise money practices.

I highly recommend that you get your money plan together prior to the wedding. Learning to "finance togetherness" is the topic of an entire book I co-authored with Greg Pettys and David Edwards, called *The Smart Stepfamily Guide to Financial Planning*. You'll get a small taste of that material in chapter 9, which might be helpful to absorb before you share any significant financial changes when children are involved (e.g., changing the names of beneficiaries on insurance policies).

Roles in the Home

While a single mother, Lavonda worked extra hours and relied on her mother to pick up the kids from school and watch them until she got off work. Her oldest daughter, Jasmine, looked after her siblings and helped make lunches for them before school. Between Lavonda, Grandma, and his big sister, Daniel, the youngest, had three "mothers" to care for him. He relished being the baby of the family and often took advantage of it. But after Lavonda married, she no longer needed to work as much, Grandma didn't see the kids as often, Jasmine lost part of her contribution to the family, and Daniel, who now wasn't the youngest child, found himself competing with a younger stepsibling for attention.

Changes in roles can be substantial for family members. In some situations, the person receives benefit. Jasmine, for example, was released of having to make lunches in the morning because her mom could now do it, but Jasmine found herself feeling less significant to the family. In other cases, the person experiences a disadvantage. Grandma, Lavonda's mother, will likely experience a loss in not being able to spend time with her grandchildren as she had in the past. But then, maybe that is a welcome relief.

Help both adults and children anticipate how their roles within the home may shift or change. If a child has fulfilled a critical role for a long time, be sure to celebrate their contributions and thank them for their service and sacrifice. If they will not be needed as they were in the past, reframe the change like a graduation or milestone birthday; that is, from this point forward, they have an opportunity to discover new roads.

Parenting Expectations

Chapter 6 gave you the opportunity to explore your parenting strategies and how you will parent together following the wedding. Now is the time to begin making small changes in that direction and informing the children of what will change. But this should not be a one-way street. Ask them questions about what they would like to see change as it relates to your parenting style and consider their input. No, they don't get to dictate how you parent or what the rules will be, but healthy parents have an ongoing feedback loop in their parenting that helps them refine their attitudes and behaviors.

ACTIVITY INSTRUCTIONS

Review each of these items first as a couple. You may have definite opinions about some of them that you need to agree on before you inform the children. But whenever possible, as much as is developmentally appropriate, let children have input. This makes it more likely they will own responsibility for implementing the solution. When you must make the call on a decision, it is helpful if you let kids speak into some aspect of the changing situation (e.g., bedtime on school nights is nonnegotiable, but on weekends is negotiable). Share power when you can.

Be as practical as you can in these conversations and explore all relevant topics. The examples below are just a few possible questions. Start by saying something like, "You know, we got to thinking about all the things that will change once we get married and move in together. Some of them are going to be welcomed changes, and others will be beyond your control. Let's try to think of as many as we can and talk about them."

1. "What's one thing you are really looking forward to? Who wants to go first?"

2. "What's one thing you aren't looking forward to? I'll go first on this one."

3. A Seismic Shift: Explain to your children that you are bringing a significant relationship into the family and you know it will bring some changes. Then reassure children that this does not mean you will stop being their parent or loving them in a unique and special way. Then, if developmentally appropriate, ask them what changes they've already noticed in how you spend your time with your fiancé and if they have felt in competition with that relationship.

   a. Parent and stepparent: Be sure to respond to children with empathy (e.g., "I can see how tough that would be for you").

   b. Parent: Resist the temptation to change the child's attitude or feelings in order to move them emotionally toward your fiancé (e.g., "You don't have to worry that I spend time with him/her"). Just listen and affirm for now. Carving out one-on-one time with your child is what will actually reassure them.

4. Routines: "Let's walk through a typical day. How do you think things will change with more people in the house? Breakfast? Getting to school/work? Evenings? Bedtime? Weekends?"

   a. "What will you miss about how things used to be?" [Sometimes this question reveals a hidden emotional anchor that you can try to replace some other way.]

   b. Remind people that a change in your time with them is not to say that they are less valuable to you.

5. Rituals, Traditions, Holidays, and Special Days: Use an upcoming special day as a case study to discuss traditions, their meaning, and how you will manage things going forward. Don't try to negotiate every tradition, just discuss a few examples and note that you'll have to figure out the specifics of each as they come up.

   a. "Lori has a birthday coming up soon. What do you guys usually do to celebrate birthdays?"

   b. "Lori, what is meaningful to you about that? What would you never want to lose?"

   c. Holidays: "Both sides of our family have a special tradition on Christmas morning. We can't do them both like we have in the past. How should we handle that in the future?"

   d. Remind everyone that your family won't get everything right the first time. "We may have to learn from our mistakes, but we will try to consider everyone's feelings."

6. Primary Residence and Physical Space in the Home:

   a. "Let's talk about how things might feel different around the house. The boys are going to share a room. What do you guys think that will be like?"

   b. Share a situation that you anticipate will change, and invite others to talk about it. For example, "On Friday nights for a long time, David (son) and I have enjoyed sitting on the couch, watching movies, and eating pizza. There will be a lot more people in the house now. David, I know I'm going to miss that alone time with you a little, but I'll enjoy having others with us too. What do you think it will be like?"

c. "With stepsiblings in the house together, it might be wise for us to have a dress code. What should that be? Under what conditions can you enter someone's bedroom? If you have a problem, who do you talk to?" (Read more about personal boundaries in stepfamilies and awkward physical touch in my book *The Smart Stepdad*.)

d. Discuss changes in bedrooms, bathroom use, kitchen use, TV/computer/media time, etc.

e. More people in the family means less time with a parent. Anticipate what this might mean for them and reassure them of the things that will continue (e.g., a special nighttime ritual with a child). Acknowledge openly what needs to be grieved (e.g., going to lunch regularly with a child).

7. Faith Perspectives: Point out your similarities and differences and discuss how you will manage them going forward. If changes need to be made (e.g., finding a church your whole family will attend), start a dialogue about what people value in a church and why.

8. School and Social Life: Because these can be so unique for children, you may want to talk with them individually but have collective discussions about how school changes will impact the family calendar.

9. Visitation Schedule and Logistics:

a. Regarding visitation, biological parents should explain any frequency or schedule changes to their children—and explain how you plan to honor the other parent's time with the child.

b. Discuss what might change in terms of logistics. For example, "We will live closer to your dad's house,

so it will take less time to get there—that's a good
thing!"

c. Talk through days when some children will be
present and some gone and how it will impact
room situations, responsibilities around the
house, etc.

10. Vacation: Start talking about your next vacation and
what people want to do. Listen to their past experiences
and what they liked. Start dreaming of what you might
do together.

11. Money and Spending Habits:

a. Tell children who they go to for lunch money or to
make college payments.

b. Explore what you anticipate changing as it relates to
the overall household income. Give practical examples of what might change. (Example: "We're going
to have a lot more kids in the house once we get
married, so all of us are going to have to limit our
outside activities to one per semester. I know that
stinks. We are giving up some things as well. What
questions do you have about this?")

c. Let children know of any negotiated changes in
how you will manage or distribute money (e.g.,
allowance).

12. Roles in the Home:

a. Start by making a quick list of how each family
member contributes to the home. Then anticipate
with the group how those roles will stay the same or
change.

b. Remember to honor people for significant roles they
have played in the past that will no longer be needed,

and celebrate their new freedoms. Be sure to also acknowledge the loss they may feel at not being able to
contribute in a familiar way.

13. Parenting Expectations:

    a. What general expectations/rules will be the same,
and which will change?

    b. What chores will children be responsible for?

    c. Explain what the kids should expect if they misbe-
have and who they will hear from.

    d. If developmentally appropriate, give kids a chance
to speak into what is expected of them. This sends
a message that you are open to (but not required to)
listening to them. Ask what rules or expectations
they would like to see change in the future (e.g.,
teenagers may want more freedom to make decisions
about their time). Note: Kids are observant. Likely
they have already experienced the differences between you as parents and have opinions about what
they like and don't like in a future stepparent. Ask
them to share their thoughts.

POST-ACTIVITY QUESTIONS FOR REFLECTION

How many new changes will your children need to adapt to?
Pause and reflect on all that will be required of them. Remember that change, especially unwanted change, brings loss and a
sense of powerlessness (for kids and adults alike) so prioritize
the changes and move slowly. To increase stability, strive to
reduce unnecessary changes for children and be compassionate when they react strongly to what is, for them, another six
inches of water.

TRY THIS

Talk with a friend about their blended family transition. What changes did they not anticipate well? Depending on their age, invite your children to talk with a friend and ask the same question. Your family might even interview another family all together so kids and adults alike hear what everyone has to say.

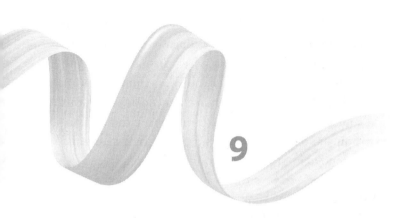

9

MERGING MONEY AND YOUR FAMILY

I was being interviewed on CNBC about *The Smart Stepfamily Guide to Financial Planning*, when the program anchor questioned something important: "Why do most blended family couples avoid talking about money?"

She was right. One study found that fewer than 25 percent of premarital couples forming blended families discussed financial matters,[1] and yet research by Dr. David Olson and myself found that happy, thriving stepcouples have an 80 percent agreement rate on spending and saving.[2] That's twice the rate of unhappy couples! Not talking about money is a bad idea, but for more than just financial reasons. Ultimately, as I'll explain in this chapter, stepfamily financial planning is about financing relational and emotional togetherness in your marriage, in your family, and on behalf of your collective financial futures.

Did you know that long after a divorce, a former spouse is entitled to a portion of your retirement and stock options?

Did you know that, unless you've made legal arrangements, if you die and your former spouse marries again—and then your former spouse dies—some of your assets can end up going to their new spouse and their children, not *your* children? What if you decide not to update insurance beneficiaries or your will and something happens, leaving someone without financial provision—and family members bickering over assets and what you intended in the event of your death?

This doesn't have to be part of your future. To avoid these difficulties, devote some time to the Growth Activity in this chapter. For a few couples, this chapter will be enough to help you create a unifying plan, but most will benefit from reading *The Smart Stepfamily Guide to Financial Planning*, which presents a comprehensive process for merging your money and your family. After doing the research for that book, I now tell premarital coaches, counselors, and pastors that I believe we have a moral obligation to push couples into this discussion because if we don't, they can get blindsided quickly. I don't want you to get blindsided. The benefits of a healthy discussion are great, and the problems avoided are many. If you find yourself a little hesitant to jump in, trust that now is the time to start the conversation. You don't have to settle all the questions, but you do need to get started.

By the way, my reply to the CNBC anchor's question about why couples often avoid talking about finances was twofold: First, because even though partners flippantly say to each other, "I'll take care of yours and you'll take care of mine," they don't really know what that means or how they'll do it. The attitude may be romantic, but their good intentions often get overrun by stepfamily realities, including legal restrictions, complex multiple-home parenting, relationship challenges, and extended family members. I shared that you need more than just good intentions; you need a plan. And second, most couples think they don't have enough money to worry about. That's not true. Everybody has something, even if it's debt. Everything matters. At this point you may have a significant retirement nest egg saved or not many assets at all, but starting to plan now will help you get your new family started off on the right foot. Remember, this conversation helps you merge more than just money. It merges your values and dreams and, most important, helps you decide how money will serve your family. I'll add a third reason pre-blended family couples avoid talking about money: They have already studied one of the many popular money management systems and feel equipped. These courses offer much, but rarely, if ever, do they talk through the unique financial issues impacting blended family couples, nor do they address relational trust issues and parenting dilemmas that can complicate or sabotage most common financial programs. Merging money and merging family relationships are always tied together in blended families. Get ahead of the game; start planning now.

On Merging Money and Family

A stepfamily is a complex spaghetti of loyalties, cultures, traditions, DNA, expectations, parenting styles, losses, fears, and people—both those in the home and outside the home. As this book has discussed, merging means attending to all these pieces.

What does this have to do with financial planning and money management? Everything. If older stepsiblings got a car when they turned sixteen, once you marry are you obligated to do the same for younger children just to keep it fair? What do you do if the other home lets your child be on a traveling sports team and then expects you to help pay for it with time and money? How many bank accounts should stepcouples have? Do you put

141

your new spouse's name on the house, or buy a different house? And what do you do, for example, if for financial and child development reasons you decide not to buy a child a smartphone, but the other home does it anyway? Are these solely money matters? Not at all. When you look underneath, it's obvious that many financial conflicts in stepfamilies are much bigger issues of belonging, loyalty, trust, power, control, acceptance, perceptions of favoritism, and fears of relational uncertainty.[3]

"My husband often spends money on his kids without discussing it with me first. He brought three children to the marriage, and they are older than my two. I just want to be included and considered. Leaving me out makes me feel unimportant, and I'm suspicious of what else he and his kids may be hiding." This woman's primary complaint is not about money; it's about trust and feeling unimportant in the marriage and, therefore, unsafe. An issue about decision-making and spending has revealed these feelings, but ultimately, this isn't about money. Said another way, financial conflicts are often just a symptom of much deeper blended family dynamics and relationships.

Below the surface. Michelle wasn't trying to shut Jamar out. Eventually, he learned more about Michelle's past and understood more about her apprehensions. Her first husband had abandoned her for another woman and left Michelle with little except debt from a stack of maxed-out credit cards. It took her many years to get out from under the constant worry about how she would pay the bills. Now, she admitted, she was guarded and cautious with her finances and children.

I've met many couples in blended families who have similar concerns. When below-the-surface issues come up, it's important for both partners in a relationship to exercise great patience with each other's fears before dealing with financial decisions. As Jamar and Michelle came to understand each other's pasts, they found compassion and grace for each other. They lowered their demands related to money and became much more patient with the merging process. Accommodating each other while they continued to work through their fears was an act of love that, ultimately, helped make true oneness more possible.[4]

Dealing with hidden issues. In any situation where there is a below-the-surface issue, seek to resolve that first, even if that means delaying a money management decision. The most important conversations you will have as a couple are around matters of commitment, companionship, and cherishing each other. In blended families, conversations may also need to address parenting and stepparenting priorities, coping with ex-spouses, and other stressful dynamics. Finding agreement about these matters while setting boundaries to protect and guard your family affirms your love for each other and raises confidence in the long-term dedication of each partner. When those below-the-surface insecurities are relieved, return to above-the-surface financial decisions and find an agreeable solution.

The necessary element of trust. With every step of this journey, each partner must act in a trustworthy manner. One woman wrote to me feeling trapped. Her husband forced her to sign a prenuptial agreement before they married without much discussion of the items included. He controlled their finances after they married and gave her little decision-making power. Then, in a move that cost him the little trust she still had in him, he set up a trust to provide for his kids but wouldn't let her speak into the details. Ironically, his financial trust came at the great cost of relational trust with his wife. Building trust between you is worth every conversation, every awkward moment, and every sacrifice. Without relational trust, your financial decisions will fail.

Stop and reflect. What are the below-the-surface issues in your relationship right now? Which of those are yours to manage and/ or change? Begin to recognize below-the-surface emotional and relational issues that must be addressed so that you can later consider the above-the-surface, practical matters of merging your financial lives.

Practical Steps to Financing Your Togetherness

How do you orchestrate a healthy family and financial merger? Here are a few practical steps discussed at length in the book *The Smart Stepfamily Guide to Financial Planning.*

Step one: take stock. Taking stock of yourself and your family relationships is an important first step to developing a financial vision for your blended family. Since stepfamilies are born out of loss (the death of a parent or the dissolution of the parents' relationship), understanding the past and your present emotional health is important in understanding how your blended family is functioning—and how well you'll be able to negotiate financial matters.

You also need to take stock of your financial situation. The Activity below will help, but for now, think in generalities: What are your major assets and remaining debts? Who are the people you are financially responsible for (e.g., children) or to (e.g., aging parents)? What happens to all of this if one of you dies?

Step two: create a Togetherness Agreement. A Togetherness Agreement (TA) helps you plan to succeed. A TA is a detailed financial vison of your life together. Essentially, it involves putting everything on the financial table—your assets, debts, dreams, and obligations—and deciding how you can meet your needs and facilitate the permanency of your marriage. This takes work, but the net result is a stronger relationship as you design your positive and secure future together.

Some will choose to have their TA drafted by a lawyer so that it is binding (a legal contract). Others will be satisfied to talk through the matter on their own (with or without an attorney) and design a path forward. Both create a shared vision for life together.

The specific stipulations included in a Togetherness Agreement vary by couple but will give consideration to your specific blended family. Your TA might include general agreements about handling finances, such as whether you will keep some bank accounts separate and have a joint account, and how you will manage retirement portfolios, debt, insurance, and businesses. It might also include agreements regarding the financial support, rights, roles, responsibilities, and overall well-being of spouses, children, stepchildren, grandchildren, stepgrandchildren, parents, stepparents, grandparents, stepgrandparents, and other significant relationships.

The TA is not just about money; it's a plan for how money will help care for your family over time. And therein lies an important attitude distinction that influences whether money matters help or hurt blended families: A prenuptial agreement is done *to* your spouse when you want to protect yourself in the event of a divorce. A Togetherness Agreement is done *for* your spouse. Better yet, when it is created *with* your spouse, both persons make promises on behalf of the other and lay a positive foundation for their life together.[5]

Negative reactions. If the idea of a Togetherness Agreement brings up a strong negative reaction in your partner or in you, consider how you might respond.

Consult with your pastor, mentor, or financial planner. Having a third party guide your discussion can be very helpful. In addition, recognize that strong reactions may be indicative of deep fears in your partner or in you. Recognize the fear and articulate it. Put aside conversations about the details of your money matters, and as a couple talk about your past experiences and what's driving strong emotional reactions now. Then you can return to making financial plans.

Below are some specific elements of the TA that you may want to discuss.

Bank accounts. Discuss how many bank accounts you'll have and who has access to the money therein. Should you have just one account that both of you have complete access to, two pots based on your differing incomes and liabilities, or three accounts (or more) with a combination of his, hers, and our money? Some people think this decision is symbolic of each person's level of trust in the other. "If she won't put all her money into our account," one man told me, "then she isn't really committed to me." Can you hear his below-the-surface insecurities? Until these are addressed, he likely won't be open to anything other than a one-account system. But know this: There are many good ways to manage your money. The number of accounts matters less than the fact that you discussed it, decided on a system that you can both support, and you feel trusted by each other. Unity does not mean one account. In this case, it means unity of heart. It's also very helpful if you have the bigger picture agreed to as well. Knowing how assets are being used to provide for both yourself, your spouse, and your children in the event someone dies, for example, means you trust the heart of your spouse beyond how many bank accounts you have.

Money boundaries with kids. Significant changes in money boundaries can, for kids, add water to their tank (see the be-

If you find it difficult to manage conflicts about money or any other subject, consider consulting *The Smart Stepfamily Marriage* by Ron Deal and David Olson, a book that helps couples develop practical skills to strengthen their marriage.

ginning of chapter 8). As a single mom, Taylor was quick to hand money to her children whenever they asked. They had been through a lot when their father left, and there wasn't much she could do about it; this felt like something she could control for them. Heading into marriage with a man who would rather give his children a set amount and see them manage it for themselves, this is a potential problem. Together they need to define how much money is appropriate to give kids, as well as how often and under what circumstances they will give it. If this changes anything for Taylor's children, she needs to be the one to communicate it.

If boundary issues like this arise during your conversation, pull back and slow down. A situation like this has many elements to it (parenting, money, family history, emotional security, etc.). Explore them together, but ultimately in a case like this, the biological parent needs to be the one making the changes with their children. This clearly communicates that the parent is in favor of and responsible for the change.

Money boundaries with a previous spouse. Let's consider another example that includes a former spouse. Victor is a successful businessman who regularly negotiates big financial deals. But ever since his divorce, he's catered to his ex-wife. In an effort to avoid conflict, he's agreed to give her more custody time and money than required by their divorce decree.

Then he married Felicia, a highly successful consultant who's not afraid of controversy. Victor and Felicia agreed that she would manage their finances. As soon as she looked at the books, she told Victor's ex that they were no longer going to give her extra money every month. Felicia was simply trying to help her new family be better stewards of their money, and she believed setting limits would help Victor's children learn to do the same. The decision sent waves crashing through the co-parenting relationship, Victor and Felicia's marriage, and

Felicia's relationship with her new stepchildren, who heard their mother's side of the story first.

The primary problem here was not whether Victor and Felicia should reduce paying for things, but that Felicia acted without first discussing the situation with Victor. Decide *together* how you will implement changes. Felicia should have seen that there would be strong feelings about finances on both sides and many layers to consider, and that there would likely be numerous conversations before they could agree on what to do. Whatever it took, finding unity would be well worth the effort because it would support their new, fragile marriage, their parenting and stepparenting, and the foundation of their home.[6]

Should your current spouse get into the negotiation mix? This is a common question for blended families who experience mid- to high-conflict co-parenting situations. (Low-conflict co-parents are generally able to talk through parenting and money issues.) Ideally, biological parents work together for their children, but sometimes they can't and the question arises whether a stepparent should step in and negotiate on behalf of their household.

Every situation is different, and that's why there's not one right answer to this question. Some couples intuitively know that involving the stepparent will make things worse. However, if the stepparent is willing to be involved and has the temperament of a mediator, give it a try. For example, if a stepdad and biological dad can have a productive discussion about between-home parenting and money matters, then the biological mom doesn't have to take part in the conversations if she doesn't want to. But she should most certainly talk with her husband before and after he speaks to her former husband.

Some stepfamilies find that this is a temporary arrangement that helps everyone through a challenging season, and others find it is a good long-term solution. In any case, it is important for the stepparent couple to talk a great deal in advance of the negotiation so the stepparent can represent their household well when talking with the other home. Once the conversation with the other home begins, the stepparent should not make any commitments before talking again with their spouse in private unless they are confident the biological parent will be okay with the decision.

Between-Home Communication Strategies That Help

When it comes to negotiations with a former partner, sometimes the outcome of a money or boundary conversation depends largely on how you start it. Having a business mentality in your exchanges can be helpful.[7]

Open with an invitation, not a demand. Instead of saying, "I need more money today to cover this," say, "Ella's travel team is adding games, and they're farther away. It's getting expensive. Could we meet to discuss her plans?" You've had time to consider the situation and arrive at the conclusion that more financial support is required; give the other person the chance to do the same. If you just declare what needs to happen, you can create a control issue. Give the co-parent a chance to think about it and process the information. At that point, a collaborative decision to contribute money is more likely.

Open with a question. "Dillon wants a tutor. How do you feel about that?" Starting the conversation like this respects the other parent's opinions and gives them a chance to process the situation. Again, you've had a chance to do that, so make sure they get to as well.

Show gratitude. Whenever possible, begin the conversation with gratefulness for what your co-parent has already done before discussing additional expenses. "I appreciate you paying for the band fee and instrument rental. I've paid for the uniform and competition travel costs as agreed. But now the school is asking we pay for the hotel at the competition." Asking for more without acknowledging what both parties have already done feels cold and is likely to make your co-parent feel taken for granted. Keeping your heart appreciative makes openness from them more likely.

"You go first. What do you think is fair?" Especially if there is friction between you, this approach changes the dynamic from one of you trying to be in control of the solution ("Here's what should happen") to one where the co-parent can take the lead and be responsible for finding what's fair. Of course, there's no guarantee their opinion will match yours, but it might at least shift the climate of the dialogue away from power and control to collaboration.

Know your triggers. It's vital you know what your personal hot buttons are, why you react the way you do with a co-parent, and how you can regulate your emotions in the midst of tension. Divorces and nonmarital breakups tempt people into viewing the other person as the bad guy and themselves as the victim. This false narrative can leave you blind to any contributions you may bring to ongoing conflict; it's easy to blame the other person and focus on their faults and totally miss your own. Managing money with former spouses starts when you look closely in the mirror, know what sets you off, and then manage yourself well.[8]

Getting Started

The Growth Activity questions below will get you started building a simple, verbal Togetherness Agreement. There isn't space in this book to explore all the topics you might need to discuss or the various financial tools and strategies available; you can explore *The Smart Stepfamily Guide to Financial Planning* or consult with a CFP (Certified Financial Planner) or estate attorney for a thorough discussion of merging properties, managing a business, insurance and retirement plans, legal issues, boundaries with adult children, and more. But for now, let the Activity get you started. Identify any emotionally charged issues for your family, affirm your commitment to the permanency of your marriage, and begin exploring how you will provide for each other and your children.

ACTIVITY INSTRUCTIONS

As a couple, first discuss some general subjects to explore your attitudes about money. Then you'll address some logistics.

1. State aloud your overall goal as it relates to utilizing money as a tool to care for your spouse, children, and stepchildren. What would you like to see happen as you walk out your marriage together? What would you like to see happen financially when one of you dies? Would you like to pursue creating a formal Togetherness Agreement?

2. Once married, how do you envision merging your assets and debt? Are there things you'd like to keep separate? What implications does this have for daily money management, paying bills, and caring for the household and children?

3. Under what circumstances can one of you spend money on, or give money to, children without the other knowing about it?

4. Some stepparents feel confused by the ambiguity of being responsible to care for stepchildren but not always being included in financial decisions that affect them (or

their biological children). It's also confusing if they are expected to financially support stepchildren but then are left out of parenting decisions that affect everyone. How might this be a factor in your marriage?

5. What spending habits of the other make you a little nervous? What habits do you appreciate?

6. How important to you is tithing to your place of worship and doing good works in the community?

7. What below-the-surface issues has this chapter surfaced for you? Make a list of emotionally charged financial matters.

Now discuss some practicalities of money management.

1. Write down everything you own and owe (assets and debts). Assets include bank accounts, retirement accounts, investments, real estate, personal property, vehicles, insurance, pensions, etc. Debts include home mortgage, vehicle loans, credit card balances, personal or consumer loans, unpaid income tax, and any other bills or debts that are not paid off monthly. Review your insurance and investment documents together.

2. Create a general plan for day-to-day and monthly expenses. Walk through a typical month as a good case study.

   a. Daily money management logistics: How do we anticipate managing day-to-day expenses, deposits, and accounting?

   b. How many bank accounts will we have?

      • Who has control and access to the funds? Who can use a debit card (or write checks), make deposits, or transfer money into or out of each account?

Who will be responsible for paying bills from and managing a joint account?

- Who gets each account in the event of a death?
- How transparent are the financial transactions? Even if your spouse is not named on an account, should you provide some way for them to see what's going on with it, through paper statements or online access?

c. Health, auto, and home insurance.

d. Parenting: Discuss, for example, how you have handled giving children money in the past and what you will do once your families merge.

e. What is your philosophy about saving for emergencies?

3. Begin estate planning. What are your general thoughts about these subjects?

a. Wills? What happens if one of you dies?

b. Investments and retirement savings?

c. Insurance beneficiaries?

d. Paying for your cars, college, and computers (devices)?

e. Social security?

f. Family business?

g. Do you expect to receive an inheritance at some point?

4. Once you agree to a general plan, how much of it do you think you should communicate to your children or

To learn more, *The Smart Stepfamily Guide to Financial Planning* discusses updating beneficiary designations, managing debt, investments, real estate, and businesses or closely held corporations, saving for college, end-of-life disability and health-care wishes, and more.

extended family? When would you like to communicate this?

a. Keep in mind that adult children often appreciate being told of any significant estate changes before the wedding—and need to hear it from their biological parent (with the new spouse present as well).

b. Older children and teens should be told about logistical changes that impact their daily lives and expectations.

TRY THIS

There are many creative financial tools that can help blended family couples provide for one another and their children. You don't have to choose between your spouse and your children. For a thorough examination of the dynamics related to money and blended families, read my book *The Smart Stepfamily Guide to Financial Planning* (co-authored with Greg Pettys and David Edwards). In addition, you can consult with a Certified Financial Planner (CFP) or estate attorney. For more, visit https://edwardsgroupllc.lpages.co/blended-family-finances.

10

TILL DEATH DO US PART

As I write this chapter, the world is in a pandemic. It's May 2021 and we're beginning to see a little light at the end of the tunnel, but we're still not sure if it's a train barreling down upon us.

In case you missed it, the coronavirus pandemic was a global pandemic of coronavirus disease 2019 (COVID-19). The outbreak was first identified in December 2019 in Wuhan, China. The World Health Organization declared the outbreak a public health emergency in January 2020 and a pandemic in March.[1] As of May 2021, more than 165 million cases of COVID-19 were confirmed worldwide, with 3.4 million people dying from the virus.[2]

I remember when I first heard about the pandemic. I must admit, I didn't think it would travel from China to the U.S. so quickly, and even then, I didn't think it would last long. And no one I spoke to thought it would either. But it did. The pandemic's impact was far-reaching, touching not just the health of millions, but the economy, political climate, work environment, travel, educational system, religious practice—our complete way of life.

A lot of us experienced a kind of shock initially once work and school began to shut down. And a kind of denial. "It can't be that bad," we said. "This will pass soon." But before long, the reality of the situation settled in and we began to adjust.

The experts told us we needed to socially distance. Work from home. Do school from home. And don't go out unless you absolutely need to. Essentially, we were told to pull back to the safety of home and be around the people we trusted most.

Social distancing and staying close to home required many adjustments on our part. Single people quickly found themselves working at home, eating at home, and existing alone. (Thank God for video calls and conferencing that kept us connected at least in some way with others.) Couples and families quickly found themselves schooling from home, working from home, and confined at home, while some children found themselves unable to be with a parent who lived in another home. (Again, thank God for video conferencing!) Parents had to figure out how to help their children do school online and work a full day, and children had to cope with not seeing their friends or having a social life. My youngest son, Brennan, had to come home from college mid-semester and do online school from our home. Boy, was he depressed! My wife and I had to deal with an angry son who invaded our pleasant little empty nest. Boy, were we depressed! Adjustments like this were happening by the thousands in real time while people were getting sick and losing their jobs. At first, it was sort of like a staycation, but then it got old . . . fast!

Couples had to regroup and figure out how they would manage their jobs, the kids, and school. Families had to learn how to share the computer, the Wi-Fi bandwidth, and the living room (I mean, the office/school room). Businesses adapted to employees working at home almost overnight. And professional sports creatively found solutions to allow the game to go on. Did this bring about frustration, irritation, inefficiency, confusion, and discouragement? You bet! And as a result, some people didn't cope well and crashed. Just a few months into the pandemic, news reports suggested that liquor sales, online gambling, and child abuse and domestic violence were up while online dating activity went down. Websites designed to facilitate affairs had increased views, and porn sites saw double-digit growth.[3]

On the other hand, others did cope well. Despite the anxiety and ambiguity caused by the pandemic, communication, flexibility, and the willingness to negotiate the new normal were the skills of the resilient. *We took a breath. Held God's hand. Faced reality. Pressed in. Managed to cope. And most of us made it through.*

The next challenge was about reopening (returning to work, restaurants, and social gatherings). Some said it should come sooner, others later, some slowly, others quickly. Social media wars and political posturing exacerbated this debate. Despite the bluster, one message was clearly communicated: To open wisely, wear a mask and remain six feet away. But putting that into action turned out to be challenging. What, exactly, is the definition of "six feet"? To some it meant an arm's length and behind a Plexiglass window. To others, it meant ten feet apart with you wearing a double-mask and they a hazmat suit. Still to others it meant "back to normal" with no distance and no mask. Clearly the process for reopening wasn't clear at all.

Again, there was public debate, irritating exchanges in the grocery store, and family arguments over if, when, and where into society people might go. I was asked to write an article for *U.S. News and World Report* on co-parenting in the midst of what I called the COVID Crazies. The central question they wanted me to discuss was what co-parents should do if they disagreed about releasing children into social situations. What one household decided would certainly impact everyone in both homes, but what if you disagreed on the definition of "six feet"?[4]

While all of this was going on, the medical community feverishly sought to create a vaccine. The world watched and waited. Reports of their progress carried hope forward even though we were cautioned there would not be a quick fix. Again, *we took a breath. Held God's hand. Faced reality. Pressed in. Managed to cope. And we made it through.*

Today, we have been forever changed by the pandemic. You or someone close to you may have been impacted by a death. Before the pandemic, my father was fairly healthy and living in an assisted living environment, but months of little physical activity and isolation (we could only visit him through video chat) escalated his decline and hid a blood cancer no one knew anything about. He never recovered. Others have been recalibrated for the better, but all of us have been recalibrated, likely in many ways. For example, you may be more aware of how fragile life can be or find yourself slightly cautious about physical spacing when in public. It could be said that we haven't fully "recovered" to life as it was—or as we thought it was going to be. But I do think we've adapted. Grown. And can enjoy life as we've come to know it.

On Pandemics and Blended Families

What does all of this have to do with your plans to form a blended family? The journey of coping with the pandemic is metaphorical to the journey the average blended family travels in becoming family. There are several parallels in the narrative—and in the coping—that you can apply and hang on to.

Have you heard? Right now, you are just starting your family journey. After reading from this book the "early reports" of what may be ahead, you might be like some who reacted with great fear to China's initial reports of COVID-19 while others thought news stories were greatly exaggerated. Either way, I suspect as reality gets closer to home, you'll want to revisit some of the principles of this book or perhaps dive into one of the other books in the SMART STEPFAMILY SERIES (see the list in the front of this book for more titles) so you know how to cope.

Social distancing. If and when stepfamily realities affect your home (in the form of predictable stepfamily dynamics), perhaps you will be like some COVID-19 patients who were asymptomatic: The effects just weren't that difficult, and they barely felt a thing. Others, however, had significant symptoms and needed serious medical attention. Most blended families fall somewhere in the middle; they do experience some distress and "growing pains" as they begin the journey to bond, discover love, and build a family identity. And when they do, most will also experience "social distancing," that is, the natural drift of biological family members (insiders) back toward the people and places that are most safe. Every stepfamily has togetherness forces and distancing forces that create a push/pull effect. As the stress of merging increases, distancing forces become stronger.

Now hear this: Just as in the pandemic, while it makes sense on some level to stop pushing people together if the virus of ambiguity wants to pull them apart, you shouldn't stop altogether. As I said in chapter 8, during times of stress, biological parents should spend more exclusive time with their children in order to reassure them of their love and presence, but that doesn't mean total lockdown from the "outsiders" in the home. Rather, become more strategic—as we did in the pandemic— about when and how to spend time around others. Yes, you may feel strangely vulnerable when doing so, but that's necessary to overcome fear of the unknown and to form trust. Social distancing is not fun, and it doesn't represent the ultimate goal (you want togetherness in your family, not separateness), but when used for strategic purposes for a season, it can serve your family quite well.

Navigating the new normal. Just as the "stay at home" mandate required parents and children to figure out how to live, work, school, and play in the same space—without outside breaks, no less—you will have to navigate the new normal for your family. The Growth Activity of chapter 8 tried to help you anticipate new routines, schedules, and how you will share physical and emotional spaces once you combine every aspect of your lives, but no one can fully anticipate this. Reality will teach you what you really must figure out.

I can imagine, just as we did in the pandemic, that you will step on each other's toes a little. Not intentionally, of course, but you will. And each of those relational missteps will give you a chance to further define your expectations of each other, what you need, and the logistics of life. This is the live-and-learn aspect of stepfamily living that cannot be avoided. But more than that, I believe, it's a necessary evil that ultimately helps bring definition to ambiguous relationships and over time helps to create rituals and traditions that form family identity. The Activities of this book have already opened the door to important conversations between family members. Continue to walk through that conversation door when life invites you to, and together, you'll co-create a familyness filled with reward.

Reopening and "six feet away." Just as not everyone during the pandemic had the same definition of "six feet away," individual members of your family may have different expectations and definitions of emotional closeness and distance. Some are comfortable being two feet away with no masks, while others want a lot of distance and hazmat suits on. Navigating each person's level of comfort and willingness to close the gap over time takes intentional communication. When you connected with a co-worker or friend at church during the pandemic, you may have greeted them with a question meant to bring definition to how you would interact: "Are you shaking hands? I'd prefer we just bump elbows." Likewise, be proactive in your family communication in order to gauge the level of openness of one family member to another. Once you get a baseline understanding, periodically check in with them to see if anything has changed. Imagine a stepdad saying, "It's okay that there's some things you want to talk to your mom about and not me. I get that. Just know I'm cool with it when you are." Proactively defining the boundaries of your relationships lets everyone know where they stand and what to expect, and gives some clarity in the midst of much ambiguity as to how they will interact.

As in the pandemic, *remember to take a breath. Hold God's hand. Face reality. Press in. Learn to cope. And you'll make it through.*

Forever changed. The pandemic changed all of us (at least a little). The journey into familyness will also change you and your family forever. (Relationships—both a vertical one with God and horizontal ones with each other—tend to do that to us.) The pain of your past has changed you and the children as well. Those recalibrations come with you into this new recalibration. The trick is embracing all of it, learning from it, and being changed into who Love would have you become in order to thrive. I doubt you will fully recover the fantasies of blended family life you began with or had before picking up this book. But I do think, in the end, you will have adapted. Grown. And can enjoy life as you will come to know it.

Turning Points

Looking back at the pandemic, we can see how individuals and our society as a whole crossed various turning points in coping with the virus. Again and again, uncertainty and stress rose, and we learned to deal with them. Some turning points we managed pretty well; some we didn't. But I'm sure in both cases we didn't have any idea we were crossing a turning point. It's only in looking back that we can see that the moment mattered and things got better.

You too will one day look back at your journey to family-ness and notice turning points—moments whose significance was hidden from you while going through them, but which you can clearly see now. For example, the moment you persevered through family conflict. You resolved the argument, but what you didn't realize is that your perseverance and communication helped engender trust between family members. A child, for example, saw how committed you were to them, and their hearts softened. Or the time you realized you were trying too hard to get your children to love your spouse, so you took a half-step back; you didn't give up, you just stopped pushing them together and controlling their relationship and gave them a little space. Years later you discovered that "grace space" allowed them to relax around each other and figure out how to take one another, in their own time, into their hearts. Or the time you were totally surprised by your stepchild. You had come to accept that your stepchildren just didn't think of you as someone they could trust deeply; they liked you, even could say they loved you, but they really didn't interact with you as a mom or dad. That's why you were caught so off-guard when you realized one day that they trusted you far more than you knew. "When did that happen?" you asked yourself. "Why did that happen?"

Most of the time you will cross these turning points that quietly and gently move your family forward without noticing. Only time will reveal how significant they were. So trust that doing the best you can with God's guidance is more than enough to bring about good things for your family. But sometimes you will notice the turning point and rejoice.

Cody noticed one and just had to share it with me. He called this turning point his "miracle weekend." Cody and his wife, Kimberly, had been married for five years. She brought four children to the marriage, ages thirty-five, twenty-nine, twenty-three, and twenty-one, and five grandchildren. Not having any children of his own, he explained in his email, led him to settle into the idea that as a stepparent, he would not get to experience many of the special parental moments that most biological parents do.

Kimberly's two oldest were married with families of their own. When Cody came into their life, they were adults and working on starting their careers and families; they didn't have much time for him. The youngest and he got along well, but the third child, a girl, kept her distance from him. Audrey was a daddy's girl. She was generally respectful toward Cody, he explained, but never really let him in. Until the miracle weekend, that is.

"This past weekend," he said, "Audrey got married. She asked me to walk her from the bridal suite to the aisle, where her father and grandfather would give her away. I never thought in a million years that I would be able to walk a bride down the aisle and was so honored to be asked. This was enough of a miracle for me, but God was not through.

"I was also asked to pick up the cake on the day of the wedding. It was about an hour drive each way, so my wife's grandson asked if he could come. I wasn't sure what his dad—my stepson— would say, but he agreed without hesitation. My grandson and I had a great time, and he later told his dad how we had wonderful bonding time.

"Then, seconds before the walk down the aisle, my wife's youngest realized she forgot her earrings and asked me to put them in for her. She actually allowed me to touch her! That trust meant the world to me.

"And then, to cap it all off, a few hours after the reception, I looked at my phone for the first time all night and there was a text from the bride thanking me for being there, because when she saw me, she said, all her anxiety and fear went away. I had choked back tears all night, but now I wept happy tears at the miracles that God put in my life that day."

Now, listen to the next part. "I never tried to be their father and never will; I just show them love and support. But I will always call them my children."

He experienced the wedding weekend as a miracle, but it was his gentle and patient approach for years leading up to the wedding that allowed that moment to occur. His stepdaughter's wedding revealed the turning points that had been happening all along.

You usually won't know you crossed a turning point until many years later, but remember, it's faithful love in the midst of the ambiguity that makes the turning point happen in the first place.

Till Death Do Us Part

Hanging on to the pandemic metaphor will give you perspective and perhaps a framework for understanding where you are in the journey. It's helpful to bring a little clarity to the unknown. But your commitment "till death do us part" is even more important. If and when the going gets tough, it will be your promise that keeps your eyes looking up, not down at the mud through which you walk. Discouragement and disillusionment may enter your peripheral vision at some point, but keep your eyes focused on your promise, your goal of traveling this life together as husband and wife.

In jest I've often said that God's little joke on us is that we make a vow at the beginning of our marriage, and then life teaches us what we committed ourselves to. You have no idea what you're really saying when you declare "Till death do us part." You don't know what sacrifices you'll have to make on behalf of your marriage, what accommodations you'll have to adopt as a stepparent, what suffering you'll have to endure as parents, or what monumental joys you'll experience as leaders of your family. But if you *take a breath. Hold God's hand. Face reality. Press in. Learn to cope. And remain committed to your vow,* you'll make it through.

May God bless your journey together.

TRY THIS

Every journey needs a map and good friends that offer support. After your wedding:

1. Pick up a map: Read my book *The Smart Stepfamily: 7 Steps to a Healthy Family*, the most comprehensive faith-based resource on stepfamily living available, and my book coauthored with Dr. Gary Chapman, *Building Love Together in Blended Families: The 5 Love Languages and Becoming Stepfamily Smart*, a book that focuses on family bonding.

2. Find some friends: Join a small group or start one yourself. Multiple video curriculum, conferences, and virtual classes for individual couples or groups, including *The Smart Stepfamily*, can be found online at SmartStepfamilies.com.

Notes

1. Most couples forming blended families don't seek premarital preparation. Fewer than 25 percent of couples in a series of studies sought relationship or educational opportunities to discuss their upcoming blended family marriage. Less than half even read a book or magazine article about remarriage or stepparenting. See Lawrence Ganong and Marilyn Coleman, *Stepfamily Relationships: Development, Dynamics, and Interventions* (New York: Kluwer Academic, 2004), 68.

Chapter 1 Not Just a Couple

1. S. M. Stanley, P. R. Amato, C. A. Johnson, and H. J. Markman, "Premarital education, marital quality, and marital stability: Findings from a large, random household survey," *Journal of Family Psychology*, 20, 1 (2006): 117–26.

2. J. S. Carroll and W. J. Doherty, "Evaluating the effectiveness of premarital prevention programs: A meta-analytic review of outcome research," *Family Relations*, 52 (2003): 105–118.

3. Brian Higginbotham, Linda Skogrand, and Eliza Torres, "Stepfamily education: Perceived benefits for children," *Journal of Divorce and Remarriage*, 51 (2010): 36–49.

4. Leslie Baxter et al., "Empty ritual: Young-adult stepchildren's perceptions of the remarriage ceremony," *Journal of Social and Personal Relationships* 26, no. 4 (2009): 467–487.

5. Patricia Papernow, *Surviving and Thriving in Stepfamily Relationships: What Works and What Doesn't* (New York: Routledge, 2013), 67.

Chapter 2 Seeing Is Eye-Opening

1. Ron L. Deal, *Dating and the Single Parent* (Bloomington, MN: Bethany House Publishers, 2012), 20, 41.

2. Ron L. Deal, *Dating and the Single Parent*, 102.

Chapter 3 Helpful Expectations

1. Ron L. Deal, *The Smart Stepfamily: 7 Steps to a Healthy Family* (Bloomington, MN: Bethany House, 2014), 99.

2. Lauren Reitsema, *In Their Shoes: Helping Parents Better Understand and Connect with Children of Divorce* (Bloomington, MN: Bethany House, 2019), 146–147.

3. For more on this, see Ron L. Deal, *Placing Your Spouse in the Front Seat of Your Heart*, 2014, www.familylife.com/articles/topics/blended-family/remarriage/staying-married-remarriage/placing-your-spouse-in-the-front-seat-of-your-heart.

4. Ron L. Deal, *The Smart Stepfamily: 7 Steps to a Healthy Family*, 93.

5. S. M. Stanley, G. K. Rhoades, and F. D. Fincham, "Understanding romantic relationships among emerging adults: The significant roles of cohabitation and ambiguity," in F. D. Fincham and M. Cui (eds.), *Romantic Relationships in Emerging Adulthood* (Cambridge, England: Cambridge University Press, 2010), 234–251.

Chapter 4 Planning Your Wedding

1. Leslie Baxter et al., "Empty ritual," 467–487.

2. Leslie Baxter, et. al, "Empty ritual," 478.

3. Leslie Baxter, et al., "Empty ritual," 477.

4. Leslie Baxter, et al., "Empty ritual," 484.

Chapter 5 Co-Creating Familyness

1. Ron Deal, "The Name Game," www.smartstepfamilies.com/smart-help/learn/parenting-stepparenting/the-name-game-dissecting-the-emotional-significance-of-names.

2. Ron L. Deal, *Dating and the Single Parent*, 212.

3. You can learn more about the "no-threat message" in the books *The Smart Stepmom: Practical Steps to Help You Thrive* by Ron L. Deal and Laura Petherbridge, and *The Smart Stepdad: Steps to Help You Succeed* by Ron L. Deal.

4. For more, read "The Name Game: Dissecting the Emotional Significance of Names" by Ron Deal, found here: www.smartstepfamilies.com/name-game.

Chapter 6 Parenting Together

1. Ron L. Deal and David H. Olson, *The Smart Stepfamily Marriage: Keys to Success in the Blended Family* (Bloomington, MN: Bethany House, 2015), 102.

2. As reported in Lawrence Ganong and Marilyn Coleman, *Stepfamily Relationships: Development, Dynamics, and Interventions, 2nd ed.* (New York: Springer, 2017), 83.

3. Ron L. Deal and David H. Olson, *The Smart Stepfamily Marriage*, 106.

4. Adapted from Ron L. Deal, *The Smart Stepfamily: 7 Steps to a Healthy Family*, 145–148. Used by permission of Bethany House Publishers, a division of Baker Publishing Group.

5. Key 1 is adapted from *The Smart Stepfamily: 7 Steps to a Healthy Family* by Ron L. Deal, 176. Used by permission of Bethany House Publishers, a division of Baker Publishing Group.

6. Dr. Susan Gamach, "Parental status: A new construct describing adolescent perceptions of stepfathers" (PhD diss., University of British Columbia, 2000).

7. John and Emily Visher, *How to Win as a Stepfamily, 2nd ed.* (New York: Brunner/Mazel, 1982).

8. Personal communication, July 27, 2020.

9. James Bray, *Stepfamilies: Love, Marriage, and Parenting in the First Decade* (New York: Broadway Books, 1998).

10. Emily and John Visher, *How to Win as a Stepfamily*, 110–112.

11. Keys 2–4 are adapted from *The Smart Stepfamily Marriage* by Ron L. Deal and David H. Olson, 106–110. Used by permission of Bethany House Publishers, a division of Baker Publishing Group.

12. Ron L. Deal and David H. Olson, *The Smart Stepfamily Marriage*, 106.

13. Adapted from Ron L. Deal and David H. Olson, *The Smart Stepfamily Marriage*, 111–113.

14. You can learn more about this parenting strategy in *The Smart Stepdad: Steps to Help You Succeed* by Ron L. Deal, 128–130, and online at www. smartstepfamilies.com/catch-them.

Chapter 7 Creating a Shared Grief Journey

1. John Gottman with Joan Declaire, *Raising an Emotionally Intelligent Child: The Heart of Parenting* (New York: Simon & Schuster, 1998), 24.

2. Adapted from Ron L. Deal and Laura Petherbridge, *The Smart Stepmom: Practical Steps to Help You Thrive* (Bloomington, MN: Bethany House, 2011), 76–78.

3. Ron L. Deal, *The Smart Stepfamily: 7 Steps to a Healthy Family*, 244–245.

4. Ron L. Deal, *Dating and the Single Parent*, 216.

Chapter 8 Anticipating What Will Change

1. Karen S. Bonnell and Patricia L. Papernow, *The Stepfamily Handbook: From Dating, to Getting Serious, to Forming a "Blended Family"* (Kirkland, WA: KDP, 2019), 50–51.

Chapter 9 Merging Money and Your Family

1. As reported in Lawrence Ganong and Marilyn Coleman, *Stepfamily Relationships*, 83.

2. Ron L. Deal and David H. Olson, *The Smart Stepfamily Marriage: Keys to Success in the Blended Family*, 192.

3. Adapted from *The Smart Stepfamily Guide to Financial Planning: Money Management Before and After You Blend a Family* by Ron L. Deal, Greg S. Pettys, and David O. Edwards (2019, 23). Used by permission of Bethany House Publishers, a division of Baker Publishing Group.

4. Ron L. Deal, Greg S. Pettys, and David O. Edwards, *The Smart Stepfamily Guide to Financial Planning*, 52.

5. Adapted from *The Smart Stepfamily Guide to Financial Planning* by Ron L. Deal, Greg S. Pettys, and David O. Edwards, 33–34, 45.

6. Ron L. Deal, Greg S. Pettys, and David O. Edwards, *Setting Financial Boundaries in Blended Families*, www.familylife.com/articles/topics/blended-family/remarriage/staying-married-remarriage/setting-financial-boundaries-in-blended-families.

7. Adapted from "How to Discuss Money with an Ex," *Money*, November 19, 2013, http://time.com/money/2794912/how-to-discuss-money-with-an-ex.

8. Ron L. Deal, Greg S. Pettys, and David O. Edwards, "Guidelines for Discussing Finances With an Ex-spouse," FamilyLife, https://www.familylife.com/articles/topics/blended-family/stepparents/multiple-home-realities/guidelines-for-discussing-finances-with-an-ex-spouse.

Chapter 10 Till Death Do Us Part

1. "Statement on the second meeting of the International Health Regulations (2005) Emergency Committee regarding the outbreak of novel coronavirus (2019-nCoV)," World Health Organization (WHO), January 30, 2020, www.who.int/news/item/30-01-2020-statement-on-the-second-meeting-of-the-international-health-regulations-(2005)-emergency-committee-regarding-the-outbreak-of-novel-coronavirus-(2019-ncov).

2. "COVID-19 Dashboard by the Center for Systems Science and Engineering (CSSE) at Johns Hopkins University (JHU)," Johns Hopkins University & Medicine Coronavirus Resource Center, accessed May 20, 2021, https://coronavirus.jhu.edu/map.html.

3. See the following articles: Robby Berman, "How do people cope with the pandemic? Survey reveals worrying trends," Medical News Today, May 6, 2020, www.medicalnewstoday.com/articles/how-do-people-cope-with-the-pandemic-survey-reveals-worrying-trends; Kaye Quek and Meagan Tyler, "When staying home isn't safe: COVID-19, pornography and the pandemic of violence against women," ABC Religion and Ethics, April 7, 2020, www.abc.net.au/religion/coronavirus-pornography-and-the-pandemic-of-violence-against-wo/12131020; Newsdesk, "Studies show dramatic rise in online gambling during COVID-19 lockdowns," Inside Asian Gaming, April 9, 2020, www.asgam.com/index.php/2020/04/09/studies-show-dramatic-rise-in-online-gambling-during-covid-19-lockdowns.

4. See Ron L. Deal, "Better Safe Than Sorry: Co-Parenting in the Age of Social Distancing," *U.S. News and World Report*, April 24, 2020, https:// health.usnews.com/wellness/for-parents/articles/co-parenting-during-the -coronavirus-pandemic.

About the Author

Ron L. Deal is a marriage and family author, speaker, and therapist. He is founder of Smart Stepfamilies™, the director of FamilyLife Blended® (a division of FamilyLife®), and the author/co-author of numerous books, including *The Smart Stepfamily Marriage*, *The Smart Stepmom*, *The Smart Stepdad*, *Dating and the Single Parent*, *The Smart Stepfamily Guide to Financial Planning*, *Daily Encouragement for the Smart Stepfamily*, and the bestselling *The Smart Stepfamily* and *Building Love Together in Blended Families* with Dr. Gary Chapman. In addition, he is the consulting editor of the SMART STEPFAMILY SERIES and has published over a dozen videos and study resources and hundreds of magazine and online articles. His work has been quoted or referenced by many news outlets such as the *New York Times*, the *Wall Street Journal*, *Good Morning America*, *U.S. News & World Report*, and *USA Today*. Ron's popular books, podcast (*FamilyLife Blended*), conference events, social media presence, online classes, and one-minute radio feature (heard daily on hundreds of stations nationwide and online) make him the leading voice on blended families in the U.S. He is a licensed marriage and family therapist who frequently appears in the national media, and he conducts marriage and family seminars around the country and internationally. He and his wife, Nan, have three boys. To connect to all of Ron's resources, go to SmartStepfamilies.com.

More Resources for the Smart Stepfamily

Visit smartstepfamilies.com and familylife.com/blended for additional information.

Providing practical, realistic solutions to the unique issues that stepfamilies face, Ron L. Deal helps remarried couples solve the everyday challenges of stepparenting and shares seven steps to raising a healthy family.

The Smart Stepfamily

This guide to financial planning for blended families offers help and encouragement as you plan your combined financial future while protecting your marriage in the process. You'll find tips on handling debt, bills, and child support from previous relationships and advice on planning for college expenses, retirement, and an inheritance.

The Smart Stepfamily Guide to Financial Planning

◊ BETHANYHOUSE

Stay up to date on your favorite books and authors with our free e-newsletters. Sign up today at bethanyhouse.com.

 facebook.com/BHPnonfiction

 @bethany_house

 @bethany_house_nonfiction

You May Also Like . . .

Stepfamily experts Ron L. Deal and Laura Petherbridge show you how to survive and thrive as a stepmom, including how to be a positive influence on the children and how to deal with conflict, as well as practical issues like dealing with holidays and between-home communication.

The Smart Stepmom

Here is the survival guide every stepfather needs to succeed. Ron L. Deal equips stepdads everywhere with advice on everything—from how to connect with your stepchildren to handling tricky issues such as discipline and dealing with your wife's ex.

The Smart Stepdad

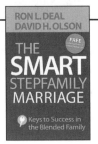

Leading blended family authority Ron Deal and marriage and family expert David Olson show you how to build on your relationship strengths and improve your weaknesses. Whether you're dating, engaged, a young stepfamily, or an empty-nest couple, *The Smart Stepfamily Marriage* gives you the tools you need at any stage to create a remarriage that will last.

The Smart Stepfamily Marriage

◈ BETHANYHOUSE